ORIENTAL
RUGS IN COLOUR

Oriental rugs in colour

by

PREBEN LIEBETRAU

The Macmillan Company, New York
Collier-Macmillan Ltd., London

This book was first published in Denmark in 1962
under the title ORIENTALSKE TÆPPER I FARVER

Translated from the Danish by Katherine John

Colour photography by Aa. Strüwing

The Macmillan Company, New York
Collier-Macmillan Canada Ltd., Galt, Ontario
Divisions of The Crowell-Collier Publishing Company

Library of Congress catalogue card number: 63—18408

Printed in Denmark
Christtreus Bogtrykkeri

CONTENTS

FOREWORD

In this practical guide I have tried to give an impression, in text and pictures, of what hand-knotted oriental rugs really are. The book gives some history, and brief accounts of a few famous rugs, but it is planned above all as a guide to the rugs most commonly seen today, and the rich traditions behind their making. This includes information on their colour, patterns, symbolism etc., together with advice on purchase and treatment. Finally, a section of the book contains individual descriptions of 65 typical, selected rugs, reproduced in colour, so that the reader may get a comprehensive idea of the whole oriental rug market today.

My warm thanks are due in the first place to the *Magasin du Nord*, Copenhagen, who made available for photography the majority of the rugs illustrated, and also to *Persisk Tæppelager, Iranske (Persiske) Tæpper (Henry L. W. Jensen)*, and *Lysberg, Hansen & Therp* who were also good enough to lend rugs.

I am indebted for very kind assistance to the library of *Kunstindustrimuseet*, Copenhagen, and for valuable information to the Victoria and Albert Museum, London, and *Österreichisches Museum für angewandte Kunst*, Vienna. I would also like to thank *Dr. Mostafa Namdar*, First Secretary to the Iranian Embassy in Copenhagen, the staff of the Turkish Embassy, and two of my colleagues in the rug trade, *Svend Petersen* of Copenhagen and *Edvard Pedersen* of Aarhus. Finally special acknowledgement is due to the distinguished rug expert, *Mr. Nils Nessim* of Stockholm, for his critical revision of the manuscript.

Preben Liebetrau

ORIENTAL RUGS

WHAT ARE ORIENTAL RUGS

The term 'oriental carpets' simply means carpets from the East, but it is usually applied to *hand-knotted rugs,* produced in the wide area stretching from the Balkans in south-east Europe, over Turkey (Anatolia), North Africa, the Caucasus, Iran (formerly Persia), Afghanistan, Baluchistan (now West Pakistan), part of India, Turkmenistan (Turkestan) and China. It is seldom possible to say exactly where a rug was made, or precisely how old it is. Tribes migrated or intermarried, and copied one another's traditional patterns. Since the end of the nineteenth century many patterns have been woven to order, in places far from their original source, to satisfy the western market. Some towns, villages or tribes who were once important rug weavers no longer make any, although the products for which they were once famous can still be bought in antique shops. On the other hand, new centres have appeared even since the Second World War, and these have often adopted for their rugs the older patterns of their neighbours.

Oriental rugs are popularly described as 'genuine' carpets though the term is hardly applicable since there are no 'imitation' rugs. But 'genuine' suggests that these carpets are hand-made and therefore individual.

It should be appreciated that oriental carpets are not just articles for use, but often works of art on a high plane, fascinating in their richness of design, their symbolism, their imagination and their delight in colour. It is not surprising that on occasion they have been used as models for machine-made carpets.

History

Where and when carpets were first knotted nobody can tell, but nomad tribesmen in Central Asia may have been amongst the first rug weavers since they had the necessary material, wool, and an incentive, a climate which was bitterly cold in winter. The first rugs were probably hides, pure and simple, and their purpose was to keep out draughts and cold. Perhaps the deerskin itself served as the model for oriental rugs with their small, knotted tufts of wool forming a pile not unlike the animal's coat.

Since the materials of carpet-making are perishable, there are natural limits to the age of existing specimens. But in literature and art we find accounts and pictures which give us an idea of how early, in the history of civilisation, oriental carpets appeared.

The earliest large group of pile fabrics to survive has come from the burying grounds of Egypt, from Akhmîn and the Faiyûm. Looped pile was used on shirts, on hangings and perhaps on coverlets, but for decoration rather than for warmth. The pile is sometimes woollen, but is generally made of shaggy linen and is looped rather differently from the true hand-knotted carpet. There are examples in museums all over the world wherever collections of Coptic textiles have been assembled, and they date from the fifth to the tenth century A. D. Although many of the more ancient civilisations of the world are known to have had fine textiles of silk and linen, it is impossible to say now what exactly these were, how they were made, or what they looked like. Certainly the idea of putting a carpet on the floor is quite new. Before the eighteenth century only the most prodigal would have worn out such an expensive purchase in this way.

A few years ago a most interesting find threw new light on the earliest days of rug-making. During excavations in a valley of the Altai range, South Siberia, in 1947-9, the Russian archaeologist S. J. Rudenko found a very well-preserved rug in a grave-mound belonging to a prince of Altai who lived in the fifth century B. C. Made of wool, a perishable substance, only chance has preserved this rug in such good condition. It would seem that the burial-mound had not long been raised when it was visited by grave-robbers. They removed metals and precious stones, but took no interest in carpets. Later on, torrents of water gushed in through the openings they had made, and filled the burial-chamber. The water turned into ice, and this accident has given us a 'deep-frozen' rug with its colours wonderfully preserved. The Altai Rug, on exhibition in the Hermitage Museum in Leingrad, measures 6′ × 6′6″ (1,83 × 2,00 m.). The design has a large, geometrical centre field, composed of squares and framed by a couple of main borders. In one of these, deer are represented, in the other,

warriors on horseback. The rug is a striking example of the high level of skill achieved in carpet-making more than 2500 years ago.

The use of hand-knotted rugs came very late to Europe. Until the sixteenth and seventeenth centuries, floors were usually covered with loose rushes, swept away when they became too filthy. Rush mats were introduced gradually. The walls of the rich were hung with tapestries

Motif from Assyrian obelisk, ninth century B.C.

for warmth and for decoration. Beds were furnished with woollen blankets and probably sheepskin or similar rugs if the owners could afford them.

The first oriental rugs were imported by Italian merchants trading with the Levant (Turkey today). Such rugs were accordingly exotic and expensive. The paintings of Simone Martini, who worked at the beginning of the fourteenth century, include an occasional Anatolian carpet, so we know that rugs were coming into Europe by then. In the middle of the fourteenth century, Nicholas di Buonaccorso painted the marriage of the Virgin taking place on a carpet with stylised animals for its chief decoration. The carpet in this picture, which is in the National Gallery in London, is very similar to a mid-fifteenth century carpet now in Stockholm. In the late fourteenth and fifteenth centuries, many different kinds of Anatolian and perhaps Caucasian carpets were imported by Venetian merchants, and they can be seen in the paintings of Ghirlandaio, Lorenzo de Credi, Carpaccio and many others. Generally these carpets are spread on the steps leading up to the throne where sits the Virgin. Since the back of the throne is often covered with the richest velvet of the period, it may be deduced that the rugs were considered to be almost equally precious. In paintings with secular subjects, oriental rugs sometimes appear as decorations hung from windows on festive occasions, but more often they appear in portraits. The subject of the portrait stands with his hand resting on the corner of a table draped with a handsome oriental carpet, and adorned with a few well chosen objets d'art or perhaps a manuscript or two. This seems to have been the most common use for a fine oriental rug until well into the eighteenth century. Italian merchants traded also with Northern Europe. Naturally, they sold fine silks but they dealt also in oriental rugs. In early Flemish paintings these are painted with great care. Memling incorporated a number into his paintings.

Henry VIII and Cardinal Wolsey were among the first in England to obtain large numbers of oriental rugs from Venice. Such carpets are shown in several portraits of Henry VIII and his court. The painter Holbein has given his name to a certain kind of carpet because it

Detail from the Altai Rug, fifth century B.C.

appears so often in his pictures. 'The Ambassadors' at the National Gallery in London shows two men leaning on a high open court cupboard covered with a fine Near Eastern rug.

While these fairly small Anatolian rugs were being imported into Europe, some of the finest carpets ever woven were being made in Persia. Under the patronage of the Sefavid dynasty, architecture, painting, ceramics and all the textile industries attained a level seldom equalled again. All the Persian arts of this period have much in common in their style, their richness and delicacy of ornament, their splendid but subtle colouring, and their complete mastery of technique. All these qualities may be seen in the carpets of the sixteenth and early seventeenth century now dispersed among museums across Europe and the United States.

Famous Carpets

One of the most celebrated is the Ardabil Carpet, in the Victoria and Albert Museum. This carpet, considered to be the peak of Persian art, was made in the 1530's for the great mosque of Ardabil in northern Iran. It measures 17'6" × 34'6" (5,34 × 11,52 m.) and contains about 33 million knots, or 340 knots to the square inch. It is woven in a lovely deep blue, and has a large medallion in the centre. This medallion is surrounded by 16 smaller ones. The corner designs are quarters of the centre medallion. There is an inscription in the carpet, which reads: 'I have no refuge in the world but thy threshold. There is nowhere to hide my head but under this roof. The work is slave to the sanctuary. Maksud of Kashan in the year 946.'

The date of the Ardabil carpet, 946, corresponds to about 1540 A. D. The difference is due to the fact that Moslem chronology begins with July 16th 622, the day of Mohammed's flight from Mecca to Medina. As it is not unusual for dates to figure in oriental rugs, a simple conversion-table is given below. The Moslem year is 11 days, or about $1/33$ of a year, shorter than our own. Thus the year 946 may be converted to our own reckoning as follows:

$$946 \div 33 = 28$$
$$946 - 28 = \qquad 918$$
$$+ \text{year of Mohammed's flight} \quad 622$$
$$\overline{\qquad\qquad\qquad 1540}$$

About 1880 the Ardabil carpet was sold by the mosque, for approximately £2,400, to an English

◆ ٢ ٢ ٣ ٤ ٥ ٦ ٧ ٨ ٩

0 1 2 3 4 5 6 7 8 9

Arabic numerals

carpet-buyer. Before its dispatch to Europe it was repaired at Tabriz. The pair to the carpet in the Victoria and Albert Museum is now in the Los Angeles County Museum of Art. This carpet is not quite complete, as parts of it were sacrificed to repair the carpet now in London, when both carpets were brought to Europe in the late nineteenth century.

The *Österreichisches Museum für angewandte Kunst* in Vienna has a famous, beautiful and unusual 'hunting carpet', with a silk pile. This carpet gives a lively and life-like picture of hunting scenes. It measures 10'3" × 22'6" (3,10 × 6,93 m.), and is said to have reached Vienna as a gift from Peter the Great to the Emperor Leopold I.

There is a famous carpet known as 'the Coronation Carpet' in *Rosenborg Castle* in Copenhagen. It is believed that this beautiful carpet was presented to Frederik III's queen, Sophie Amalie, in 1666, by the Dutch East India Company. It has foundation of cotton, with the design knotted in silk, and the ground, all one colour, of gold thread. It was used at the coronation of Frederik IV in 1699, and at those of all the later absolute kings.

This carpet is also described as a 'Polonaise Carpet', though it has nothing to do with Poland. There is an old belief that the carpets of Persia's great period were made in Isfahan, chiefly to order for Polish customers. We know that in 1601 the Polish king, Sigismund III, sent an Armenian trader to Kashan in Persia, so that he might superintend the work on carpets commissioned there. Several of these carpets displayed the arms of aristocratic Polish families, and from this many people assumed that they had been made in Poland. However, there is no doubt that many 'Polonaise Rugs' found their way to the various princely houses of Europe as gifts from the Shah of Persia. An oriental carpet still ranks as a 'princely' gift, and is often presented to the eminent on special occasions.

It was not until the end of the last century that oriental rugs became widely known and treasured,

partly due to the Viennese Exhibition of 1873, and the improvement of communications with the East. This trend has continued, and it is striking to observe the increasing interest in the hand-made carpets of the East shown by our industrialized rocket-and-atomic age. Many goods are now produced on the conveyor-belt, and completely standardised, but not oriental rugs. Although types, patterns and colours may be more or less determined within their geographical carpet-areas, no two carpets are completely alike. The human element leads, consciously or not, to just those irregularities which contribute to the charm of hand-made rugs.

ORIENTAL RUGS OF TODAY

The five main groups

For convenience it is necessary to find a method of classifying oriental rugs. They could be grouped according to design: medallion, hunting, vase and flower rugs, rugs of geometrical design, and prayer-rugs. Another method would be by producer: whether the rugs were made by nomads, or by semi-nomads stationary in winter, or in workshops by craftsmen leading a settled life.

Since the most usual method of classifying rugs is, however, by their place of origin we shall use it here.

Rugs can then be placed in the following five main groups:

1. The *Iranian* (Persian), the largest and most important group.

2. The *Turkoman* group. These are the popular '*red*' *carpets,* com-

prising the *Turkoman, Afghan* and *Baluchistan* rugs made in Central Asia.

3. The *Caucasian* (Russian) group, with geometrical figures for their main decoration.

4. The *Turkish* (Anatolian) group. This type of carpet is now rare in our part of the world.

5. The *Indian, Pakistani* and *Chinese* group.

Wool, cotton and silk

There are natural and good reasons why hand-made rugs should have found their home in the East. The Near East, meaning in this context Turkey and Iran, is a tableland broken and encircled by mountain-ranges, the home of nomads with camels and large numbers of goats and sheep. Sheep and goats are the most important sources of carpet-wool. Cotton is used too, for it is widely cultivated both in Iran and India. Silk from China should also be mentioned.

The nomads use wool both for the warp-and-weft threads forming the foundation (the warp threads running vertically through the carpet and the weft horizontally), and for the pile. These all-wool rugs are inclined to give a little in use; they may slant and go bumpy. Rugs from the Turkoman district of Central Asia also have a woollen warp. In workshop rugs (see page 15) a foundation of cotton is usual.

Wool is a splendid material, the best for rug-making. However, the quality varies greatly. For one thing, the sheep of cold mountainous country give a better wool than do sheep grazing the warmer valleys. The different parts of the sheep also determine the quality of the wool, the shoulder giving the best wool, the longest in fibre. Moreover, the finest wool is that yielded by lambs from eight to fourteen months old.

After the sheep have been clipped, the wool must be carded and spun. Usually the spinning is done by hand, chiefly for lack of modern spinning-mills, but also because handspun wool is the best for rug-work.

The warp and weft threads of the foundation must be firmly and strongly spun, and here long-fibred wool is commonly used. If the foundation is cotton, it will very likely be machine-spun.

The twist of the wool varies with its intended use. If it is to be used as pile-yarn, it is always more loosely spun. This has the advantage

that it can be dyed more thoroughly, and that the knots plump out like little shaving-brushes when the pile-yarn has been tied round the warp.

Rug-dyeing

The yarn is first rinsed for half an hour in hot water. If the wool is very greasy, approximately 3 % soda and a little soap are mixed into the water. Then the yarn is steeped for about 12 hours in an alum-bath, to a formula of one pound of yarn to $1/4$ pound alum. The alum-bath is then repeated, or the yarn is boiled for about an hour in alum-water. These preliminary processes must be completed before dyeing, which will take more or less time according to the particular dye. The yarn remains in the dye-bath for many hours, sometimes for days. Finally it is dried in the sun.

In the case of town or village-made rugs, yarn can be dyed in bulk so as to obtain a uniform tint. Nomads, however, constantly on the move, and with only a few primitive and small vessels at their disposal can dye only small quantities at a time, and have really no chance of hitting exactly the same shade each time. Again, there may be variations in colour because the wool comes from different sheep. Yet in nomad rugs, this very diversity of tint is often prized.

Skill in dyeing is a prerequisite for the creation of a really fine carpet, since the number of colours often increases with the density of the knotting. The dyer's craft is regarded as a science, and the carpet-dyer as a sage, to be consulted about many things. When he is at work, however, only carpet-dyers may speak to him!

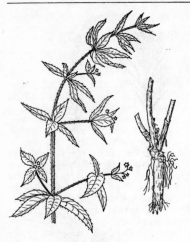

Madder plant, stalk and root

Colours and their meaning

The craftsman has a good selection of dye-stuffs at his disposal, and in the old days he had the great advantage that the material for their extraction – plants, roots and insects – could be found at his doorstep.

The red colours most frequently seen in oriental carpets are taken partly from the roots of the madder plant *(rubia tinctorium)*, a wild perennial growing to more than three feet. The dye-stuff is extracted from plants between three and six years old.

There is also *cochineal,* used for carmine red, which consists of the bodies of the female insects of the *Coccus cacti.* A third shade is derived from the insect *Chermes abietis.* Ox-blood was formerly used for reddish-browns.

Yellow is otained from the stalk, flowers and leaves of a reseda plant; saffron-yellow from the dried pistils of the saffron crocus. Today this kind of crocus is rare and therefore very expensive, so that only small quantities are used. Yellow can also be obtained from vine-leaves and pomegranate skins.

Blue is made from the indigo plant, growing in the East Indies. For green, yellow and blue are mixed.

Shades of grey and brown are obtained either by the use of natural, that is undyed, wool, or by dyeing the yarn with stuffs extracted from nutshells or oak-bark.

Finally, black may be obtained from oak-apples. It is not much used, however, because if the dye contains a lot of iron oxide, the wool fibres may go brittle. That is why oriental rugs of some age are often threadbare in the black parts, giving an unintended relief effect.

In 1856 the English chemist Sir William Henry Perkin discovered the first aniline dye, a shade of purple. After that the range of

Branch of reseda plant

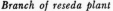

13

aniline dyes was soon extended to include red, blue, green, pink and other colours. These new dyes quickly found their way to the East, where they were welcomed since they made dyeing quicker and easier, and thus cheaper as well.

However, the first aniline dyes were not suitable for rug-yarns. They were very crude, and faded rapidly. These drawbacks naturally brought the rugs into disrepute, and caused an alarming slump in exports, especially from Persia.

Therefore, in 1903, the Persian government stopped the import and use of aniline dyes. It is said that the law was rigorously enforced, that if a dye-house was found to be using anilines, it would be razed to the ground, and that a weaver using aniline-dyed yarn might have his right hand cut off; the effect of that can easily be imagined!

Thus carpet-wool was once more dyed in natural colours, and in the period from 1903 to the First World War no synthetic dye-stuffs for rugs were used in Persia, though they were employed in neighbouring countries.

However, between the wars chemical dying made great progress, and today dye-stuffs from Western Europe, mainly Swiss and German, are used all over the East in addition to natural dyes. Nowadays there is no need to worry about synthetically dyed rugs; modern dye-stuffs are fast and have a beautiful gloss.

To the Eastern mind, every colour has a meaning. Since the Prophet's coat was green, that colour is regarded as sacred, and no true

Saffron crocus, and stalk of indigo plant

Moslem will use it as a principal colour. To Chinese, Iranians and Indians white is the colour of grief, where the West uses black. To the Iranian, blue is the colour of heaven. In Mongolia, blue stands for authority and power, red for wealth and joy. In China, yellow was the Emperor's colour, in which he dressed. To the Moslem, orange represents devotion and piety.

The Oriental has great skill in the mixing of colours; a dyer's recipes are passed on from generation to generation, and surrounded with great mystery.

LOOM AND KNOTTING

The loom

All rugs produced in the East are hand-made, and in all the great carpet-regions the technique is more or less the same; only the knots vary.

Before going on to study the weaving of the rug, we must look at the loom itself. It appears at its simplest among the nomads. Their loom consists chiefly of two beams between which the warp-threads are strung. The loom, lying flat, is held firm by pegs driven into the ground.

This narrow horizontal loom is easy to transport which is convenient, for the nomad family is frequently on the move to new and better pastures. The whole loom, perhaps with the beginnings of a rug and the remaining warp-threads can simply be rolled up, and is fairly easy to carry on camel or muleback. But of course there are limits to its size, and so nomad rugs are nearly always small.

Another type of loom is used in the town workshops which work to order, unlike the nomad weavers. This loom is upright, and consists of two strong beams, connected by two vertical posts to make a steady frame. Often the two cross beams are adjustable, to permit the weaving of rugs varying in length. If the loom is not provided with a cloth beam on which the finished part of the rug can be wound, it is very difficult for the weaver to reach the row of knots on which he is working as he proceeds further and further up the rug. To overcome this problem the plank on which he sits can be raised until

the weaver is right up against the ceiling.

The warp threads are stretched between the two beams, and are evenly spaced and regularly spun so that the pile forming the surface will also be even.

Knotting

At either end of the rug there is often a tapestry woven or 'kelim' border (see p. 19). After that the weaver begins to tie his rows of knots. These rows form the layer of pile, also called the nap, in and of which the pattern is made.

Often big balls of the yarn used for the pile are arranged according to colours, and hung on the top beam so as to be within easy reach.

When a row of knots has been tied across the whole rug, an ancient and simple tool is used; this is an instrument like a comb, of wood or iron, with which the row of knots is forced down. Then two, three, or four weft-threads are inserted, and pushed firmly down onto the woven part of the rug. The quality and stability of the foundation is determined by the number of weft-threads. A fresh row of knots is then tied, and the process continues

Weaving tools: beating-comb and knife

Upright loom with half-finished rug, showing weaving draft in the middle and weaving tools at the foot. (After A. Achdjian 'Le tapis').

until the rug has been completed. It ends as it began, with weft-threads forming a border without pile. Lastly, the loose warp-threads are knotted into a fringe.

Rug-making is hard, time-consuming and exacting work, done best by women. Perhaps they have more patience than men; they have at any rate slimmer and suppler fingers. Practically all nomad rugs are made by women, often with children to help; it is not uncommon for a woman to work with two children on each side of her. In this way they pick up the secrets and subtleties of rug-making as if in play.

On the other hand, in the regular town workshops, which may hold up to twenty looms, men and women work together. Here the weaving is directed by a *salim,* as he is called, who recites or monotonously intones the design being copied. Or again, the design may first be set down in colour on squared paper, each square indicating a knot. The weaver follows this coloured chart much as the pianist follows his sheet-music.

Beautiful results are only obtained through exact and careful workmanship. A workshop rug is never improvised, but is carefully thought out and well prepared. This does not apply to nomad rugs, where the weaver can improvise as he works; sometimes, however, the outline of the design is sketched on the warp.

A good craftswoman can tie 6,000 to 10,000 knots a day, according to the density of the knots and the nature of the material. A workshop hand commonly turns out rather more, up to 14,000 knots a day.

Examples of weaving drafts (Shah Abbas patterns)

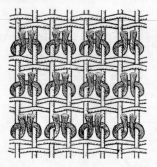

The Ghiordes knot (the Turkish knot)

The average woman weaver can tie 800 to 1,000 knots an hour. In other words, it takes her only three to four seconds to make a knot. If we assume a working day of eight hours (and in many cases it is certainly longer), that gives us an estimated 6,400 to 8,000 knots per day. Since rugs often have about 320 knots per square inch, it is easy to understand that many weeks' work may be needed for a single carpet. The largest and most complicated will occupy months or even years.

When the knotting is completed, several finishing processes are necessary. The yarn-ends forming the pile, and thus the pattern, have been cut to different lengths; to make the pile equally deep all over the rug, it must, therefore, be trimmed with special shears.

Rug-washing

The next thing is to wash the rug. This process is important to bring out the lovely lustre characteristic of oriental rugs. It can be rather a problem in the East, where many places are short of water. Some-

times, therefore, the carpet is only roughly washed and brushed, and left to dry in the sun.

Incidentally, it is now common for oriental rugs to be washed in Europe. London, Hamburg and Vienna all have big wash-houses where chemicals are employed to give the rugs a lustrous and silky finish. The washing is directed and supervised by chemists, in an atmosphere of profound secrecy. It causes the rugs to shrink a little, but also makes them denser and firmer.

Forms of knotting and weaving

In the East, in addition to *kelim-weaving* (see opposite), two kinds of knots are employed, the *Ghiordes knot* and the *Senneh knot*.

The *Ghiordes knot* (or *Turkish knot*) is more or less confined to the Near East, that is to Turkey an to the Caucasus. It is made by looping the knot round two warp-threads (the threads running lengthwise in the foundation), and bringing the ends of yarn, the pile, out between them (see drawing).

The *Senneh knot* (or *Persian knot*) predominates in Central Asia and the Far East: in Afghanistan,

The Senneh knot (the Persian knot)

India, Pakistan, Turkmenistan and China. In Iran both knots are used, according to the origin or site of the tribe or town producing the rug. The Senneh knot is made by passing the thread under one warp-thread and then round over the next, so that a pile-end shows between every warp-thread (see drawing). The Senneh knot can be made to face either left or right. In modern rugs it is not unusual to save materials and time by making the knots round four warp-threads instead of two. This 'Jufti' knot is quicker to tie but makes an inferior rug.

Kelim-weaving

The word *kelim* is Turkish and means 'Prayer-rug'. It applies to rugs which are not knotted, but woven without a pile. In kelim or tapestry-weaving the threads forming the pattern are woven across the warp, not from edge to edge, but only where pattern and colour make it necessary. Thus the weft never goes right across the rug. On the other hand, the threads forming the pattern are beaten so close that the warp-threads are practically invisible. There are small gaps, parallel to the warp-threads, where the different colours meet, unless the wefts are hooked around one another or adjacent warp-threads.

Kelims are usually rather thin and soft, and are used in the East not as floor-carpets, but as curtains and sofa or divan rugs.

Polonaise technique

The original Polonaise rugs (see p. 10) were made in the first half of the seventeenth century, usually on a foundation of cotton with a silk pile. The pile forming the

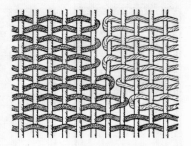

Kelim-weaving

design is tied in Senneh knots, and the ground, all one colour, is brocaded with gold or silver threads. Only very few of these rugs are preserved, most of them in museums.

However, at the beginning of the present century a small number of these rare and costly rugs began to be made in Kashan. Their gold or silver threads, inserted in the style of a kelim, are, however, not genuine gold or silver as in the old days, but mere glittering tinsel. Occasionally we come across one of these new products in the West.

Names and design

With the exception of nomad rugs the name of an oriental rug usually refers to its geographical place of origin. Since nomads are always on the move with their herds, and frequently crossing frontiers, it is often difficult to attach a place-name to their work, so that in certain cases their rugs are known by the names of their tribal groups.

The designs of oriental rugs are generally based upon a central field framed in borders, which may consist of a broad main border with lesser stripes on each side. The field

Diagrams of prayer-rug (with 'mihrab'), medallion rug and medallion rug with corners.

may have a centre pattern on a plain-coloured or floral ground, and a corner pattern, which will frequently be one quarter of the centre pattern. In other cases, the centre pattern may be split up into various main patterns, often linked by vine-tendrils.

The Moslem prayer-rug, which includes a 'prayer-niche' (a mihrab; see ill.) is an exception. The niche must always point towards Mecca when the rug is in use. The mihrab, which reappears in the Turkoman rug, can have many different shapes, and is often stepped in form. A true Moslem is loth to part with his prayer-rug. But nowadays many of the rugs from Afghanistan and Baluchistan, for example, which show some form of prayer-niche were made for export.

PERSIAN OR IRANIAN RUGS

Iran, the land of the lion and the sun, is a large country with a small number of inhabitants, numbering about nineteen millions.

Persia has been known for centuries as the wonderland of the *Thousand and One Nights;* in our time yet another wonder has been added, in the form of oil. The Persian people have always been outstanding craftsmen, with a highly developed artistic sense.

In Iran, carpets are made both in urban shops and by nomads scattered about the country. Every rug-weaving family has its original patterns, every district its characteristics, its own style.

In Iran it is quite common to see the whole floor covered with rugs.

This applies even to very modest households, but there the quality of the rugs may be inferior. There is an old proverb in the East: 'The richer a Persian, the finer his rugs.' It is still common for Iranians to invest their money in rugs, which, if necessary, can always be turned into ready cash. One might almost say that rugs are the Iranian's stocks and shares. True, he gets no annual dividend, but rugs can be re-sold at any time, frequently at a profit. This is partly because we in the West are often prepared to pay more for an old rug than for a new one, and so many old rugs have found their way from bazaars all over the country, and especially from Tehran, the capital, to buyers in Europe and America.

Since the rooms in Iranian houses are mostly rectangular, and the early rugs were made not for export but for local use, these rugs are often long and narrow, frequently composed of small patterns lengthwise.

In Iran the rugs are often arranged in the room according to a definite system. There is a central rug known as *Mian Farsh,* usually 5 to 6 yards long and about 5'11" to 8'3" (1,80 to 2,50 m.) wide. Then follows the *Kellegi* or principal rug, usually 9'11" to 11'9" (3,00 to 3,60 m.) long and 4'10" to 5'11" (1,50 to 1,80 m.) wide. These two are flanked by a couple of others, the *Kenarehs,* measuring about 5 to 6 yards by about 1 yard.

This method of covering the floor with rugs instead of using one large carpet has one great advantage. The owner can move into smaller or larger rooms without changing his rugs.

In the old days, every large household would have its own weaving-shed. Rug-weaving was not for domestic use only; rugs were also used instead of money, even for paying taxes.

Until the end of the last century, Iranian rugs were usually long and narrow, partly because of the shape of the rooms, but undoubtedly also because so many of them were produced on the narrow nomad loom (see p. 15). Conditions have changed, and today about 65 % of the rugs from Iran are workshop-made, while only the remaining 35 % are produced by nomads.

In Iran, rugs are also used as decorations at public festivals, at

Traditional arrangement of Iranian rugs

21

times even to deck the houses, as we ourselves put out flags and banners. The mosques always have lovely rugs, many of them gifts from rich benefactors.

Rugs play a very important part in the Iranian's daily life. We have already mentioned the prayer-rug, used by Moslems when the muezzin calls to prayer from the top of the minaret. This rug has the practical function of protecting the worshipper from dirt. While repeating his prayers from the Koran, he bends down and touches the rug with his forehead, placing his hands on either side of the prayer-niche, the *mihrab*, which must face towards Mecca. Mohammed imposed this ceremony five times a day: at sunrise, at midday, four hours after midday, at sunset, and about one hour later.

According to the Prophet, every Moslem should at least once in his life go on a pilgrimage to Mecca, the town where Mohammed was born in 570 A.D. In Mecca is a large square building known as the Kaaba. Built into its eastern corner is a black stone, probably a meteorite, which, according to the legend, Abraham received from the archangel Gabriel. Pilgrims walk seven times round the Kaaba, kissing the stone each time. Squares in prayer-rugs may well be symbols of the Kaaba stone.

Many prayer-rugs are very finely and densely knotted; often they are made of silk or very fine wool.

Materials

The materials used in Iranian rugs are wool, cotton and silk, though some Baluchi tribes use goat's hair to finish off the selvages at the sides

of the rug. Camel-hair is hardly used any more.

Some of the finest carpets of the 'golden period' in the fifteenth and sixteenth centuries were made on a silk warp, while the pile was frequently woollen. However, silk rugs are still being made, and what is more, made of silk produced and spun in Iran. The finest and most expensive Iranian rugs are knotted on a foundation of silk, with a silk pile. The result is an extraordinary density of knots, up to 770 knots per square inch.

Silk rugs are made chiefly in the Kashan district. They are not very good as floor covering as the material is too cold and hard. In Iran, the silk rug is used mainly as decoration, for example, on walls or tables.

Cotton is grown in Iran on a large scale, and though the fibres are of a rather short staple, they provide both warp and weft for many workshop rugs.

A cotton foundation makes the back of a rug firm and even, so that the rug lies smoothly and flat on the floor. It also has the advantage of shrinking evenly and uniformly when washed which as a rule prevents the rug from buckling.

For the coarser and cheaper rugs some of which are made in small villages, hand-spun cotton is often used since it is cheaper than the factory product. Sometimes, it is also used for strong warp-threads in urban (or workshop) rugs.

In the past, much factory-spun cotton was imported from India, but now the picture has changed, and since the Second World War a number of cotton-mills have been built in Iran. These are situated in the famous rug-areas, which are

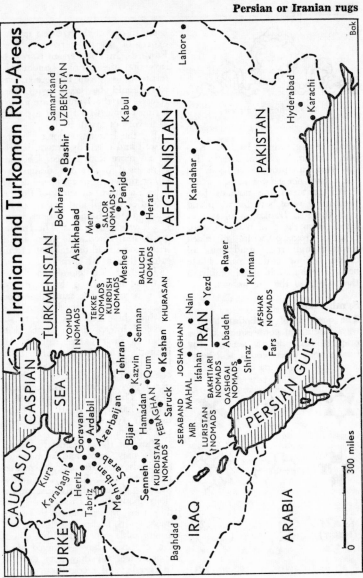

Iranian and Turkoman Rug-Areas

Cloud-band pattern

also cotton-growing: Isfahan, Kashan, Kazvin, Yezd and Tabriz. Today Iran can produce and spin all the cotton needed for rugs.

For centuries the nomads have been using wool both for warp and weft threads. Iranian wool is produced from sheep of many colours, ranging from off-white to black through numerous gradations of cream, yellow and brown. These natural colours add considerably to the palette of the rug weaver.

Symbolism

The question of symbolism has always fascinated connoisseurs of the oriental rug. Before we go any further, our wisest course will be to listen to one of the greatest modern experts on oriental carpets, A. Cecil Edwards. In *The Persian Carpet* he says that the various symbolic interpretations given by foreign writers should be taken with some reserve, for the Iranians are an art-loving people who regard a pattern as a work of art in itself.

For the Iranian, as long as a tree is well and correctly drawn, it need be no more than a tree. The patterns used in Iranian designs are either drawn from nature – a tree, a leaf, a flower or spray of flowers, a bird or animal and so on – or are adapted from foreign sources, mainly Chinese and Arabic. The Iranian artist has combined these motifs with geometrical or arabesque forms into a style of his own.

The fact that 'cloud-bands' (see ill.) and birds from the Garden of Eden occur at the same time does not mean that the Iranian borrowing these patterns accepts the mystical interpretation attached to them in their native country. He is simply using the patterns because he likes them since they have become traditional features in his design repertoire after many centuries of use. The final result which these artists have in mind is beauty through symmetry and harmony, and nothing more.

Many of these geometrical ornaments may have had a meaning hundreds of years ago, when they were first used. But it is doubtful whether there was anything mysterious about them. In all probability they were meant simply to be animals, fruits, plants and flowers, and innumerable repetitions throughout the centuries have changed their appearance, till they may now be stylised beyond recognition.

Stars and rosettes in Iranian rugs

To bear this out, Edwards suggests that the nomad woman crouching over her horizontal loom is more likely to draw inspiration from her surroundings, from what she sees, than from the abstract world of ideas.

Thus we have every reason to treat with a certain reserve the various interpretations and analyses of the Iranian rug. However, many who have studied the symbolism of oriental rugs take a different view, and the symbols as generally explained are given below.

With the Iranian, flowers have always been a favourite and principal theme. Has not the Persian garden been likened to the Garden of Eden? Stylised flowers often occur in the rugs, and here the *chrysanthemum* and the *lotus-flower* are said to mean happiness and fertility. The *iris*, which appears in the finer Iranian rugs and in a few nomad rugs, represents religious liberty.

The *rose* is also a favourite pattern, but it is difficult to reproduce. To the Kurds of West Iran, four roses together symbolise the tree of life. Further, the *tree of life* stands for divine power, a long life, or even life everlasting. The tree of life, the sacred tree, is a very ancient symbol in the East.

The *palm-tree*, which is useful to the Iranian, means the fulfilment of secret wishes; it can also mean blessing. A *weeping willow* symbolises sorrow and death.

Many of the twirls connecting the larger ornaments in Iranian work are probably reminiscences of the *cloud-band pattern*. As already mentioned, the craftsman is often inspired by his surroundings, taking his patterns from nature: *sky,*

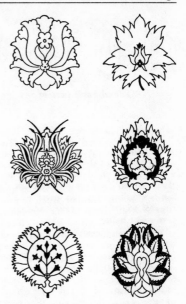

Shah Abbas patterns (palmettes)

clouds, lightning and various animals. One may also find objects for use, such as *lamps* (the sacred lamp of Mecca), *vases* and *combs*. Animal motifs are found in a wide variety of oriental rugs, from the nomad rug to the finest luxury carpets. A *dog* is often explained as the sacred dog which preceded Mohammed into Mecca. The *cock* is the devil, woven into the rug to protect its owner from the evil eye. Beasts and birds of prey, such as *lions* and *falcons*, indicate courage, victory and glory. The *heron* symbolises long life, and the *hawk* victory. The *comb* means cleanliness, while the *sword* stands for supreme power.

Several variations of the pine or leaf pattern (Mir-i-bota).

Patterns

Shah Abbas, one of the best and ablest rulers of Iran (1586-1628), was a great builder and patron of the arts. In Isfahan he established big workshops of his own where rugs of marvellous beauty and texture were made.

Various patterns bear his name, which has come to signify an important group of ornaments all inspired by the lily. These are now found in many different and complex elaborations. Often they occur in the central field of the rug, isolated from each other, yet gracefully and harmoniously linked by tendrils. Today, these patterns are made all over the country, and are familiar to all weavers whether in Kirman or Kashan, Isfahan or Tabriz.

The *pine or leaf pattern* (see ill.) is another favourite and charming design, frequently occurring, with variations, in Iranian rugs. The Iranian name for it is *bota* or *Mir-i-bota.* Though its origin is obscure, there are many interpretations of this particular pattern. It was used over and over again in different forms in shawls, first in Persia, then in Kashmir, and finally all over Europe. The 'Paisley' pattern is descended from this motif, once a graceful floral stem with a slightly bent head, now a stereotyped and rather squat bundle of meaningless ornament contained within the outline of a bent tear-drop.

A third very common ornament is the *Herati pattern* (see ill. p. 116), wich is found in rugs from practically all over Iran. It consists of a diamond-shaped central figure framed by four slightly curling leaves. The pattern varies widely in size, and is usually repeated throughout the central field. This Herati pattern is prevalent in rugs from Senneh and Kurdistan and, last but not least, from Feraghan in Central Iran. Owing to the frequency of its use in the Feraghan district, it is also known as the *Feraghan pattern.*

A similar pattern, *Mina Khani,* is often seen in rugs from Iran, especially Kurdish nomad rugs.

In Kirman it is not unusual to find portraits knotted into rugs. There are examples of European celebrities being immortalised in this way; thus we have Napoleon, Frederick the Great and a pope, all in one rug. Often shahs or wealthy men of Iran are portrayed in carpets of exceedingly skilful workmanship.

Watteauesque pictorial scenes and ancient Assyrian motifs also appear in these carpets.

The Iranians, as we see, often depict living creatures, men as well as animals, although the Prophet forbade it. This is because the Shiite branch of the faith, to which they belong, is not so strict as the Sunnite sect, which has many adherents in the Caucasus, Turkey and Iraq.

THE TURKOMAN GROUP

One principal group of oriental rugs, very widespread and popular, is the large group of *red carpets,* which may be roughly divided into *Turkoman, Afghan* and *Baluchi* rugs.

These rugs are made in the large area bounded by the Caspian Sea in the west, part of the Soviet Union in the north, Iran in the south, and Tibet in the east, and are the work of nomads who, especially in the old days, had two main pursuits, raiding their neighbours and sheep-breeding. In the mountains their herds are composed of sheep, cattle and yaks.

The Turkoman tribes are chiefly horsemen, and they have had a tradition of rug-making for centuries. The Italian traveller *Marco Polo,* after his visit to Turkmenistan in 1280, gave a glowing account of the beautiful, densely-knotted rugs.

Turkoman rugs

All purely Turkoman rugs, made by nomads or semi-nomads are familiarly described as *Bokhara rugs.* Now and then one of them is described as a *royal* or *princess* Bokhara. Nobody quite knows why – perhaps to make it more interesting, and accordingly dearer.

Though the rugs are named after Bokhara, they are not produced there; the town is merely a centre for collection and export. The name therefore, gives no clue to the tribal areas from which they derive.

Red is the predominant colour, though in many shades, right through from scarlet to wine and liver-colour.

Turkoman rugs, and indeed Afghans as well, have been made on the same principle for centuries. One essential reason for the red ground-colour is that the nomads, who still make most of them, have fewer resources than the Iranians, for example, and are mainly dependent upon red dye-stuff obtained from the madder root (see p. 13).

Example of a Turkoman 'gul'

Another reason for the deep, sombre colour of Turkoman rugs is that the Turkoman tribes, being daily exposed to strong sunlight, feel the need of a dark colour to rest their eyes.

The basic motif in the design of any Turkoman rug is the octagon or 'gul'. Formerly each tribe had its own quite distinctive variety, of which the *Tekke* is probably the most easy to recognise. On a small rug or tent bag there may be only three such guls with appropriate borders at the top and bottom of the rug. In a large carpet there may be a number of rows. Within the

Turkoman 'gul'

octagon there may be compartments which are white, blue, yellow or brown. This colouring is also found in the main and secondary borders, but nevertheless the total effect of the rug is always red.

The nomadic tribes of Central Asia who produce the Turkoman rugs, and who, with their big flocks of sheep, are always on the move in search of suitable pastures, live on the great plains stretching eastward of the Caspian Sea, and bounded by the Soviet republic of Turkmenistan (still Turkestan to rug-fanciers). Further east is the Soviet republic of Uzbekistan, with Bokhara as its capital. Further to the south-east we reach Afghanistan with its capital, Kabul.

As mentioned before, these nomad horsemen used to supplement their income by attacks on unguarded caravans or travellers. As they have never had much idea of geography or frontier posts, the treasured rugs would be made now on the Soviet, now on the Iranian or Afghan side of the border. In the old days a great many of them arrived in Europe via Meshed or Bokhara. Today, rugs woven by the more stationary nomads of Turkmenistan go through Moscow.

About twenty-five years ago one of the nomadic tribes, the Tekke Turkomans, who are considered the best rug-makers, removed their tent-poles from Turkmenistan to the northern steppes of Iran, where they are still following their traditional craft.

Turkoman rugs are usually made by women. They are famous for the high quality of their workmanship, which can be seen on many objects intended for domestic use; camel-bags, saddle-covers and door-curtains, and of course rugs for the floor of the hut (or tent) and for wall-tapestry.

In summer the Turkoman herdsman leads a pleasant life in the pastures with his flocks. There he lives in his round *kibitka*, a kind of tent, made of a wooden framework covered with felt mats. There is a special carpet for the doorway which often has a couple of hanging-straps at the top. The pattern is divided into four parts by a cross. These four fields very often display candlestick ornaments. The carpet, which is called a *Kachli*, is easy to recognize (see plate 41).

Candlestick ornaments from a Turkoman rug

Hanging on the walls inside the tent are a number of double rugs, consisting of a woven back and a knotted front. This is the Turkoman's 'chest of drawers', where he keeps his domestic articles and tools. The 'drawers' are known, according to size, as *Torba* about 15″ × 39″ (0,40 × 1,00 m.), and *Juval* about

2'7" × 5'3" (0,80 × 1,60 m.) (see plates 38 and 46 b).

As well as the octagons already mentioned, many Turkoman rugs display a stylised tarantula in their design – a large spider whose bite is dangerous to man, and which is, therefore, woven into the rugs as a means of protection.

Today, the territories of Central Asia producing most of these Turkoman rugs belong to the Soviet Union. As a result the rug trade has become a monopoly. The same cause has led to a proportion of the rugs being produced on what may be called a workshop basis.

Though the form of the patterns and the quality of the materials are the same, the new rugs are seldom as attractive as the old. Their colouring is harsher, and the patterns lose their distrinction from being frequently reproduced on a much smaller scale.

A rug woven in the same region, also by nomadic Turkomans, is the *Beshir* (or *Ersari*) *rug*. Here again red is the dominant colour. Yellows are also used, however, and on occasion greens.

Beshir rugs are often decorated with small, regular, geometrical patterns, such as stars and diamonds. One may also find Beshir rugs with S-shaped patterns, or cloud-bands scattered all over the centre of the rug. Between the bands are small geometrical figures. Finally, we occasionally see Beshir rugs with an octagonal figure in the central field.

Afghan rugs

Of all oriental rugs Afghans are surely the easiest to recognize. They are made chiefly in Afghanistan, which lies south of Turkmenistan,

Tarantula pattern

and is inhabited largely by nomadic tribes.

In Afghan rugs the ground-colour is nearly always red. However, the red varies a great deal. The older Afghans are frequently copper-coloured, while the newer ones are a deep wine red. Their patterns are usually composed of large distinctive octagons or guls which are treated very boldly. The general effect is very dark with the gul divided into four by blue and brown panels, the colours matching in opposite corners.

The rows of octagons are often set close together along the rug, while across it there may be a small stylised pattern carried out in blacks, blues and browns. Round the field are a number of borders which may sometimes be cream or white. These light colours may also appear in two of the octagons.

At first glance an Afghan rug with these light colours may suggest a Turkoman rug (see p. 27), but

Tarantula pattern

the knotting is a good deal coarser, and the pile is not cut so close as in the more expensive Turkomans.

Afghan rugs have become very popular because they have pleasant and beautiful colours, and are both hard-wearing and reasonable in price. Like the Turkomans they are very well suited for a modern house.

Afghan gul

Afghan gul

Afghan rugs are always knotted in wool and often have long fringes. Some of them have a narrow kelim border at both ends. There is a great difference in colour and density between washed and un-washed rugs, a fact which should not be overlooked.

Afghan rugs occur in many sizes, from baby Afghans of about 2'7" × 4'1" (0,80 × 1,25 m.) up to really large carpets which may be more than 5 yards long.

Baluchi rugs

Where the beautiful, primitive-looking Baluchi rugs really come from is a question which has never been settled. Of course they are generally supposed to come from Baluchistan, the country east of Iran and south of Afghanistan which is now part of West Pakistan. But the fact seems to be that the boundaries of the region where carpets are made are quite fluid, and

that most of them are probably made by Baluchi tribesmen in Northern Khurasan.

There is an old Moslem saying that at the creation of the World Allah made Baluchistan out of the bits and pieces that were left over. So it turned out a gloomy wilder-ness, and the scenery is reflected in the rugs, with their dark, sombre colouring of brown and beige; though dark reds with an occasional white motif are also characteristic.

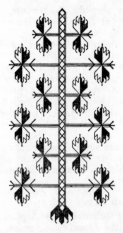

Stylised 'tree of life' from Baluchi rug

These rugs are produced by about a dozen nomadic tribes. Each tribe has its own distinctive pattern, but the colours are the same.

Baluchis, like nearly all nomad rugs, are knotted on a woollen warp, and the pile is always strong and often lustrous. As already mentioned, some Baluchi tribes use goat's hair to finish off the selvages on the sides of the rug. There is a considerable demand for Baluchi rugs both in Europe and in the United States, partly because of their moderate prices, and partly because their patterns and colouring are relevant to contemporary taste.

Meshed, in the north-east of Iran, is one of the main collecting centres for Baluchi rugs.

CAUCASIAN RUGS

Caucasian rugs come from the mountainous region between the Black Sea and the Caspian. In 1813 it was conquered by the Russians; before that it belonged to Persia.

In the course of time many different peoples have settled in the Caucasus; Turkoman tribes from Central Asia, Turks, Persians and Armenians. Part of the effect has been to make it a region of many different tribes and tongues. Yet in spite of this, Caucasian rugs have many features in common, whether they were made north or south of the mountains which divide the region. Its inaccessibility has helped the region to preserve its traditional patterns and colours.

The Turkish knot (Ghiordes knot, see ill. p. 18) is used everywhere, and the rugs are usually knotted on a foundation of wool, more rarely of cotton.

The dominant colours in Caucasian rugs are red, blue, yellow, green and ivory; some brown is also used. The patterns have a definite geometrical tendency. The main features of the design form a coherent pattern, while the minor patterns have no connection with one another (see plates 47-53). Stars, squares and swastikas form a large part of the decoration. It is not unusual to come across flowers, animals or human beings. These are also geometrical in design, very angular and hard to identify. In a Caucasian rug, the lovely, delicate flower-tendrils and patterns of Iran have become severe straight lines.

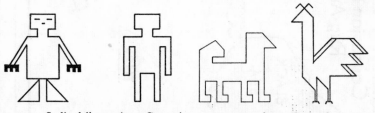

Stylised figures from Caucasian rugs: men, a dog and a cock.

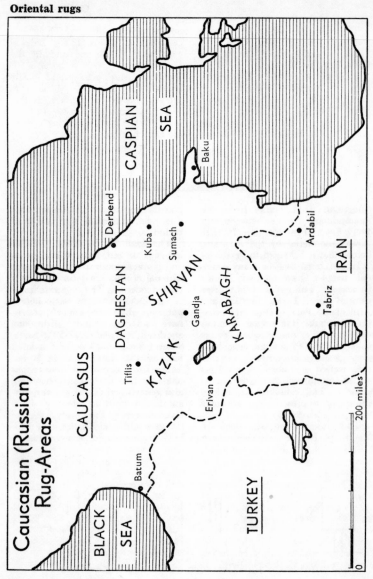

Caucasian (Russian) Rug-Areas

BLACK SEA

Batum

TURKEY

CAUCASUS

Tiflis

KAZAK

Erivan

Gandja

DAGHESTAN

SHIRVAN

KARABAGH

Derbend

Kuba

Sumach

Baku

CASPIAN SEA

IRAN

Ardabil

Tabriz

200 miles

Nowadays production is carried out in a highly standardised form. There can be little doubt that it is extensive, and that a large proportion of the rugs are sold within the Soviet Union. However, quite a number of the new rugs find their way through Leningrad – and in some cases through London – to various European countries.

These new rugs are of good quality, the knotting is regular, and the wool excellent. The design is often composed of the traditional stiff, angular, geometrical patterns. But there is a slight decline in variety and richness of colour, and the rugs are not as beautiful and well-designed as they used to be.

ANATOLIAN RUGS

'Anatolian' is the label given to rugs from the country now known as Turkey, which the Greeks and Turks used to call Anatolia. Rugs were made in Turkey as long ago as the twelfth and thirteenth centuries. The earliest patterns were either geometrical or composed of highly stylised animal forms, but in time these gave way to richer and more imaginative floral designs, for the Ottoman Turks were strongly influenced by Persian art from the fifteenth century onwards.

Anatolian rugs were imported into Europe before Persian carpets. They had a powerful influence, therefore, on the design of early European, especially Spanish, carpets. So widespread was their influence that, until the eighteenth century, upholstery made of hand-knotted pile was always referred to in England as 'turkey work'. The first European paintings showing Persian and not Turkish rugs draped on their tables date from about the 1630's onwards. Nevertheless, all through the seventeenth and eighteenth centuries many charming Turkish rugs are shown enhancing the furnishings of their owners.

The origin of a Turkish rug may often be difficult to establish, though most rugs come from the two central provinces of Ankara and Konya. Many, however, reveal Persian or Caucasian influence. At the end of the nineteenth century Turkish carpets were exported to Europe in thousands, often under the name of *Smyrna carpets*. Smyrna – or Izmir, as it is now called – was the collection and despatch centre for rugs made in the interior. The Smyrna carpet, which furnished many a respectable home, was rather coarse. Typical features were the light grey or cream ground, and the floral pattern in pink and green.

Another well-known rug is the modern *Oushak* carpet, with a bright red ground and a green and blue pattern; even the fringe is sometimes green. This design, particularly favoured for dining-rooms and libraries, has also been copied in linoleum, and, as such, has covered the floor of many cafés and restaurants in Europe.

It is very rare to find an Anatolian rug displaying men or animals, since Moslems are forbidden by the Koran to depict living creatures.

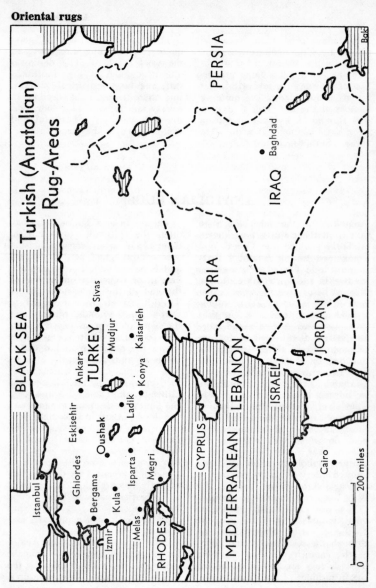

Turkish (Anatolian) Rug-Areas

BLACK SEA

PERSIA

Baku

IRAQ

Baghdad

SYRIA

TURKEY

Sivas

Ankara

Mudjur

Eskisehir

Kaisarieh

Konya

Oushak

Ladik

Ghiordes

Isparta

Bergama

Megri

Kula

Izmir

Melas

Istanbul

CYPRUS

MEDITERRANEAN

LEBANON

ISRAEL

JORDAN

RHODES

Cairo

200 miles

0

34

The Sunnites in Turkey observed this rule more strictly than the Shiite sect in Persia.

The dominant colours are red and blue. Green, a sacred colour is normally found only in prayer-rugs and in recently made carpets. Prayer-rugs have always been important in Turkey, and in the eighteenth and nineteenth centuries especially a very large number of beautiful and exquisite prayer-rugs were produced.

Turkish prayer-rugs are usually made of very good wool. The colours, although bold and bright, have something solemn about them. A rug like this has been called 'a prayer in colours'.

1922 was a black year for the Turkish rug. For in that year the creator of modern Turkey, *Kemal Ataturk,* exploited his recent victory in the Greco-Turkish war by deporting about two million Greeks, of families which had been settled in the country for centuries. Many of them spoke nothing but Turkish, and thought of themselves as Turks. It was a tragic exodus when these Christian Greeks were brutally expelled and deported to their original country where language and customs were quite strange to them.

This event is important to the student of oriental rugs since the Greeks of Turkey, with usual Greek diligence, made most of the rugs. On their disappearance from Asia Minor a vital element was lost to the Turkish craft, and this has not been made good. Nowadays, very few carpets are made in Turkey. Their quality is mediocre, and they are not often seen in the European markets.

The Greeks who returned to the land of their fathers were not exactly welcomed with open arms, since they caused the Greek Government a big employment problem. During the last few years, however, Greece itself has been turning out handmade rugs, concentrating on very robust types which can be made to order. As the industry is subsidized by the goverment, it can offer these hand-made rugs at very reasonable prices. The number of knots and depth of pile are both standardised. Unfortunately, these rugs have in general a lack of charm and individuality which are not quite compensated for by their great durability.

In addition to the rugs woven with pile, the Greeks are now making rugs based on traditional peasant designs in pattern and colour.

INDIAN RUGS

In the middle of the sixteenth century the Great Mogul Emperor *Akbar* had skilled weavers brought from Persia to India to establish rug-making. The weavers were installed in his own palace, and their task was to make rugs equal to the Persian ones. It was not long before other Indian princes borrowed the idea, and also sent for Persian weavers. For several centuries Indian rugs were, therefore, very like Persian ones both in design and colour.

The most distinguished Indian rugs were made in the reign of the splendour-loving *Shah Jehan* (1628–1658), who built the famous monument Taj Mahal. Rugs were also made to order with European arms incorporated in their design. Two of the best examples of this period are the carpet belonging to the Girdlers' Company of the City of London, and the Fremlin carpet in the Victoria and Albert Museum. Export on a large scale only began at the end of the nineteenth century. As the trade grew in importance, designs, colouring, quality and price were adapted to the demands of the European buyer.

Nowadays a large number of rugs are exported from India, where they can also be made to order. As a result a great many of the Anatolian rug-designs, for example Smyrna and Oushak, are now being copied in India; often, it must be admitted, in rather poor qualities. The weavers fetch their wool from a central warehouse, and return to their villages to make the rugs according to the instructions supplied with the materials.

The wool is usually dyed at the distribution-centre, which deals with large quantities at a time to ensure uniformity in the finished rugs.

However, there are instances in which the weaver of the rug has dyed the wool himself. Often he dyes only a little wool at a time, so that the colouring may be uneven.

The quality of the rug is determined by the type of wool. A short-staple fibre is less serviceable than a long-staple fibre. Jute is used as a foundation for the cheaper rugs.

A distinction is made between hand-spun and factory-spun yarn. Hand-spun yarn has a strong tendency to moult and fluff. As the rug-dealer would say, 'there is a large pile-shed'. In cheaper qualities the pile may be shed for years.

Immediately after the Second World War cheap Indian rugs were exported on a large scale. The quality was regrettably inferior, their pile being very coarse and stiff, in the cheapest types mixed with jute, and the colours very crude.

In India, rug-making is chiefly a man's job, though it is not uncommon to find young girls at the loom as well. Often four to six workers sit in a row, weaving the same carpet. Opposite is a foreman watching the whole carpet. He has a weaving draft on graph paper in front of him, and dictates to the weavers which colours to use. Each knot is entered on the draft in advance, in the exact shade required for the carpet.

When they have finished their work, the pile is too deep and irregular, and has to be trimmed. Usually one to two inches are cut off, according to the desired depth of pile. This job is performed not by the weavers, but by specially trained craftsmen who clip the pile of the rug little by little, till it has an even surface and a completely regular appearance.

In Indian, and still more in Chinese rugs we sometimes come across a particular kind of raised or embossed effect in the pile. This effect is obtained by another process carried out by special craftsmen; with delicate, sharp-pointed scissors they snip little grooves round the patterns, making them appear to stand out. Embossing is seen not only in patterned but in self-coloured rugs, which may, for instance, have a key pattern border clipped round the edge. This type of border is common in Chinese rugs.

PAKISTANI RUGS

West Pakistan is bounded by Iran and Afghanistan in the west, by Kashmir in the north, by India in the east and by the Arabian Sea in the south. The population is Moslem, and hand-knotted rugs, mostly in the Persian style, are made in Lahore and Karachi, though there are some examples of Caucasian or Turkoman influence. Many of these rugs are very closely and regularly knotted; the wool is handsome and lustrous, indeed often silky.

The wool used as pile is very thin and fine, and not very hard-wearing. Pakistani rugs are often knotted on a factory-spun wollen warp, and the pile is evenly clipped. The woollen fringe is a weak point in these rugs; it often wears out quickly. Karachi rugs are usually considered rather better than those from Lahore. But neither Indian nor Pakistani rugs have the charm or imagination of Iranian work.

It is fairly certain that Pakistani rugs, whose prices are kept low by a government subsidy, will become increasingly common in Europe. They are, after all, hand-knotted, and from the East.

Pakistan did not develop a rug industry of any size until after the Second World War. The rugs are woven chiefly by Moslem craftmen who left India for West Pakistan on religious grounds.

It may be added that the authorities do all they can to control production, and have introduced standard qualities. Here, and for that matter also in Iran, European carpet-firms can have rugs made to order.

The so-called *Numdah rugs* are made in Kashmir. These are neither woven nor knotted, but are felt rugs embroidered with flowers or animals. The colour of the ground is cream or black. They are remarkably cheap and very decorative.

CHINESE RUGS

No Chinese rugs earlier than the eighteenth century are known to survive, but there has been little change in the decoration or the technique used since then.

Today, the principal centres of rug-making in China are Patow, Peking, Kalgan, Shanghai and Tientsin. Tientsin is the main port from which rugs are exported.

In the province of Shantung, famous for its raw silk of the same name, rugs are made of both silk and wool; in the native land of silk it would naturally be used for rug-making.

Patterns and symbols

The patterns used by the Chinese in their rugs are much older than the technique, and are not peculiar to rugs as in other countries. Instead, they borrow motifs which are familiar in the decoration of porcelain, lacquer, jade, bronze and ivory.

The patterns seen in the older Chinese rugs are often symbols with a particular meaning. They may be divided roughly into three groups; ancient Chinese symbols in general, and the two religious groups, Buddhist and Taoist.

Many Chinese rugs are built up

Different versions of the Chinese character for 'happiness' (shou)

on a strictly geometrical scheme. In the middle of a plain central field is a medallion, often composed of meander ornaments, flowers or the character for happiness *(shou)*. Often the corners have triangular ornaments based on the same pattern. In the borders the so-called T-patterns, and also meander ornaments are common.

The swastika was not an invention of Hitler's, but is one of the most ancient and widespread symbolic devices in the world. It occurs, for instance, in India, Greece and Central America, and even in Europe during the Bronze and Iron Ages.

In some cases the swastika appears alone, in others as a link in the border-pattern. Many meanings are ascribed to it; it is said to symbolise long life, or the heart of Buddha, or the number ten thousand.

Certain small, round emblems often appearing in the borders are characters symbolising good luck like the *shou*.

Buddhists and Taoists, unlike Moslems, have always been free to depict men and animals. In addition to living forms, the Chinese include in their decorative schemes a wealth of ideographs.

Certain groups of symbols and patterns are especially popular. These are *the eight Buddhist emblems: the wheel, the parasol, the canopy, the lotus-flower, the conch, the vase with the water of life, two fish and the everlasting knot.*

The lute, the books, the chessboard and the paintings represent the four fine arts.

The eight Taoist symbols are: the sword, the gourd and crutch, the lotus-flower, the flute, the bamboo tube and magic wand, the fan, the castanets and the flowerbasket.

Various objects are known as 'the hundred precious things', among them vases, pitchers, paintings and tea-kettles.

The creature appearing most frequently in Chinese rugs is the dragon, symbolising a benevolent

Swastika pattern

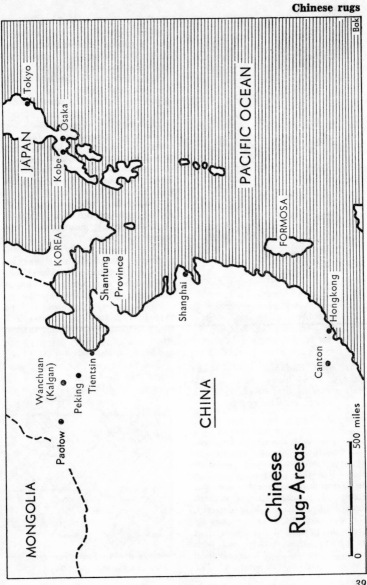

Chinese
Rug-Areas

The eight Buddhist symbols: the canopy, lotus-flower, parasol, vase with water of life, conch, two fish, wheel, everlasting knot

phoenix symbolised the empress, and is also an emblem of immortality, and brings good tidings to men from the eight protective genii.

The *elephant* is the emblem of strength and power, the *deer* of affluence, and the *crane* of longevity.

Occasionally the *horse* also appears in old Chinese rugs. If there is only one horse, it is probably white, meant as a symbol of the horse which, according to the legend, carried the Buddhist scriptures from India to China. The *lion* is another Buddhist emblem; originally it guarded Buddha, and ranks as the special guardian of the temple.

The *bat* is a lucky creature or emblem, since the Chinese word for it, *fu,* can also mean happiness. The *fish* is used as a symbol of happy marriage, and so is the *butterfly.*

Floral patterns are less stylised than in Persian rugs, so that it is easier to identify the different flowers.

The *lotus* is the holiest of all

power. Both in Europe and in Asia the dragon has always had an outstanding role in popular superstition. To the Chinese he is no wicked monster; he rules over the forces of nature, and is revered accordingly. After a long drought, for instance, the dragon comes up from the bottom of the sea or river to provide the parched soil with rain. In the old days he symbolised the authority of the emperor. The

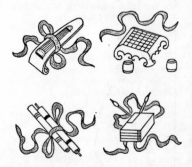

Symbols of the four fine arts: the lute, chessboard, paintings, books

The eight Taoist symbols: the sword, gourd and crutch, lotus-flower, flute, bamboo tube and magic wand, fan, castanets, flower-basket

flowers – the flower of Buddha; it represents purity and summer.

The *peony* stands for rank and wealth; it is the favourite flower of the Chinese, who love painting it and often adorn their homes with it.

The *daffodil* is used for decorating the house, especially at New Year, since it is an emblem of winter, and will bring good luck in the year to come.

The *peach-blossom* stands for spring and longevity, or even immortality.

The *pomegranate* represents fertility.

Now and then we find a composite design of floral patterns, medallions and figures, and flowers in pitchers and vases.

Colours and production

In old Chinese rugs the colouring is subdued. The ground is usually blue and yellow, in many shades. Yellowish-brown and plum-colour also occur. Reds and greens seldom appear in the old rugs. Often there are several shades of the same colour; it is not uncommon, for instance, to find a rug with three different blues in it.

Old Chinese rugs in many lovely designs are still on the market, but they are not cheap. On the other hand new Chinese rugs can now be bought at very moderate prices. Though the wool used for the pile is coarse, the rugs are certainly hard-wearing. Chinese rugs have never been very closely knotted, but they are very even. They are distinguished by their deep and strong pile; it may vary from one to two inches.

The production of modern Chinese rugs is highly standardised. There are various qualities, depending – as always with oriental rugs – partly on density of knots, and partly on depth of pile.

The new rugs show the usual Chinese colours, blue, gold or rose; though there are some in which green or beige is dominant. Generally they are designed with a central pattern, corner patterns and a border.

In Hong Kong there is a very

large concern turning out hand-made rugs in great quantities on an industrial basis.

It is considered to be the most up-to-date workshop for hand-made rugs in the world.

BUYING A RUG OF YOUR OWN

Quality and price

Since the end of the Second World War prices of oriental rugs, the better qualities in particular, have been rising. One reason, of course, is a higher standard of living in the East; the question of working hours versus leisure has arisen, and the craftsman's wages have gone up (this applies to workshop-made rugs). Competition from oil companies, contractors and engineering works in need of labour has also been felt, and former carpet weavers have been attracted to these new industries.

In Europe, London is the principal centre of the market in oriental rugs; there are big warehouses in the Port of London with rugs stacked knee-deep on every floor. Next comes Hamburg, which has built up a considerable rug-trade since the war. Zürich and Stockholm should also be mentioned as distribution centres. Leningrad is important because of its export of Russian (Caucasian) rugs. New York is probably the most important centre of the trade in the U.S.A.

Many things may determine the price of a rug; an 'expensive' name is no guarantee of quality. Even if two rugs come from the same district, there may very well be a great difference in their value. The quality of the wool and the dyes may be responsible for this, and there is also the human element; all weavers do not have the same artistic talent, or work with the same care.

In order to assess an oriental rug, one must study the wool of which it is made, and the pattern and dye. The number of knots, their fineness and regularity must also be taken into account. Finally, the general condition of the rug should be checked to see that it lies smoothly, is straight, and that there are no serious faults in the weaving.

Afghan rugs, especially, often have a rather dull and slightly dusty appearance; these are unwashed rugs. Here we must emphasise that washed rugs are more expensive than unwashed.

Advice to the purchaser

'Hassan, give me the yardstick.'
'Which yardstick, master? The one we use for buying or the one we use for selling?'

The purchase of oriental rugs is less risky at home than it can be in the East, if we may credit this brief exchange at a rug-dealer's.

The following points should be born in mind when choosing an oriental rug. First of all: do you like the rug, is it attractive? Next: will it harmonise with its intended setting? And finally: does it cost more than you had planned to spend?

An old rug is usually more expensive than a new one; and in addition some worn patches may be expected. Nomad rugs, especially, are rather apt to go bumpy or curl at the edge.

These defects can be remedied in many cases. Wrinkles can often be removed from the rug by stretching it. If the edge or corners turn over, a strap or a slip of cardboard should be sown to the back. It pays to have this done by an expert.

The wise buyer will always go to a carpet-firm, or to a shop he can trust. The rug should be seen spread out on the floor, so that wrinkles and irregularities can be discovered. Repairs can be detected by looking at the back. However, there is no need to be put off an oriental rug because it is mended; they often are. One has only to check whether the mending has been neatly and carefully carried out, and if not, to have it improved. It is also the back which shows up the regularity and density of the knots, which affect the value of the rug.

Moths are attracted by oriental rugs, but their attacks can be averted by spraying with a DDT preparation. There is usually no risk of moth in a shop-bought oriental rug, since these rugs are moved about so frequently that the moths do not find them a desirable residence.

An oriental rug may – though very seldom – be brittle or rotten. As a sign, the warp-threads will snap if the rug is vigorously folded right side out. Of course, a rug unable to stand this test is greatly reduced in value.

It goes without saying that if one can find an oriental rug without a blemish – a rug lying smoothly on the floor, with no irregularity at the edges, no bumps, holes or repairs (don't always believe the rug-salesman's romantic statement that the holes, if any, were made by sword-cuts!) – well, then it is the best, but it will be priced accordingly. And as we said, anomalies of colour and form can have a charm of their own. Yet, even in the matter of price there is a lower limit which should not be crossed when choosing an oriental rug. This limit is known to the experienced and conscientious salesman, so his advice should be taken seriously.

Oriental rugs can also be bought at auctions, though the buyer should be especially vigilant, and take care to examine the rugs before the sale if it is possible to do so. A rug sold by auction has to be taken as it is. It cannot be returned, even though faults may subsequently appear which were overlooked on the day of the sale. Another drawback is the fact that the rug cannot be taken home on approval so that one can see how it looks in the place intended for it. A reputable firm will usually agree to having the rug of your choice – or a small selection – sent to you on approval.

Have you room for a 'Dozar'?

In the rug world various sizes have their names, which it may be quite amusing to known:

Qali: a rug usually measuring 5'11" × 9'12" (1,80 × 2,80 m.) and over.

Kellegi: a long, narrow rug; usually two to three times as long as it is wide: e.g. 5'11" × 16'4" (1,80 × 5,00 m.).

Kenareh: a runner, also known as a 'strip', which is about a yard wide and from 8 to 20 feet (2,50 to 6,00 m.) long.

Dozar: a rug of bow-window or

sofa size, measuring about 4'3" × 6'11" (1,30 × 2,10 m.).

Zaronim: a small rug, measuring about 3'5" × 5' (1,00 × 1,50 m.).

Zarcherek: a bedside size, about 2'4" × 4'7" (0,70 × 1,40 m.).

Pushti: a small bedside rug, usually about 2' × 3' (0,60 × 0,90 m.).

Yastik: Turkish name for a small bedside rug, usually 10" to 1'3" (0,25 to 0,40 m.) wide and 1'8" to 2'7" (0,50 to 0,80 m.) long.

Be kind to your rug!

If you have a good, hand-knotted oriental rug at home, you must realise that you posses a work of art of high quality. Be kind to it; it deserves it!

When the rug is used on the floor, always make sure that the floor is even and has no rough patches; if it has, an underfelt is necessary. The use of underfelt saves the rug from incessant crushing between the hard floor and still harder shoe-heels.

The fringes are a vulnerable point in all oriental rugs, and they should be secured, if necessary, either by stitches at the back, or by sowing on a matching binding. Then at least the fringe can wear out by itself, without fraying the rug.

In some cases the binding has been glued on; this is naturally quicker than sowing, but it is really a pity to daub glue on a hand-made rug.

Rubber soles, especially ribbed ones, are bad for pilecarpets. The effect is much as though you were to rub your face with india-rubber! Stiletto heels can also be harmful, and heavy furniture crushes and marks the pile; it is advisable to use protectors under the legs.

Cleaning should be a gentle process. An oriental rug must not be vacuum-cleaned too often or too vigorously. A powerful modern vacuum-cleaner should never be used more than once a week, and even then, if you are very anxious to spare the rug, the nozzle should be held a little way from the surface, to avoid chafing. And you should clean only in the direction of the pile, always *with* the pile (you can establish the direction of the pile by passing your hand lightly across the rug). A gentle brushing is often enough anyway.

If the rug seems to need more thorough treatment, this should be given in winter with newly fallen snow. Spread the rug out on the snow, back uppermost, and pat it carefully, so that the pile sinks in. When it has been patted all over, pick it up and shake off the snow. If necessary, this procedure can be repeated. The rug must not get thoroughly wet, and it must be quite dry before it is walked upon again. You will be pleasantly surprised to see how lovely and lustrous it has become – and no less surprised to see how grubby the nice white snow has become. Apply this treatment every two years, or perhaps yearly if there is enough snow, and you will be doing what you can towards preserving the beauty of the rug.

A hand-knotted rug should never be beaten with a stick; the knots may come loose. Discreet use of a carpet-beater is preferable. Even then the rug must be beaten with immense care, and on the back, so that the dust and dirt are beaten out of the rug, and not down into the foundation.

The rug should be laid so that the light strikes into the pile in order to get the full value from its colour and depth.

One secret of the big difference between the look of a worn oriental rug and that of a worn factory-made rug is that when the pile of the machine-made rug has worn down, it usually reveals dull and ugly ground-threads, whereas the pile-threads of an oriental rug are looped round the warp-threads, and the actual knots are the same colour as the pile.

If the fringe of an oriental rug has started to go, it can be fairly easily repaired, and the rug is little the worse for it. It is sheer common sense to waste no time in having this done before the carpet begins to lose its pile at the raw edge. The first signs of any defect or wear in the rug itself should also be promptly treated.

When oriental rugs are being stored, they should always be rolled up against the pile, preferably on a straight stick without splinters. The folding of rugs may damage the foundation and crush the pile. If the rugs are to be stored for long, they should be wrapped up (newspapers will do) as a protection against moth. Alternatively they can be wrapped in a piece of cotton or linen (an old sheet or table-cloth), though one must be sure that the material has no holes in it. It is a good idea to brush the rug thoroughly before it is wrapped, and possibly to spray it with a DDT anti-moth preparation. While in daily use a rug is unlikely to be attacked by moth.

A rug on the wall

A small oriental rug on the wall can look remarkably pleasant and decorative; however, to get the right effect it should be hung on a plain wall, off-white or eggshell-coloured. The way to fix the rug without damaging it is as follows. A sleeve is made from a piece of material sown on the back, just below the fringe at one end. Both the upper and lower edges have to be stitched, but not through the rug, only to the back. When the sleeve has been sewn on, a bamboo rod is pushed through it; the thickness of the rod is determined by the weight of the rug, and the rod can be made four to six inches longer than the width of the rug. The rod with the rug hanging from it is placed across a couple of nails or hooks in the wall, and that completes the arrangement.

Thus we avoid wear and tear of the rug, at the same time imitating the Oriental who often makes use of rugs as wall-decoration.

This method is especially advisable for a fine silk rug which you are anxious to preserve, or for a worn, antique rug.

An oriental rug takes a long time to wear out. In fact you could almost say that one rug may wear out several generations. In the contemporary world this mixture of strength and beauty is welcome; surrounded as we are by perishable mass products, we are drawn towards the pure and genuine art of the handicraftsman.

One often hears people say that oriental rugs 'never wear out'. This is of course an exaggeration, and threadbare specimens are easy enough to find, especially among older rugs. A distinction is made between antique rugs (over 100 years) and semi-antique (50 to 100 years). However, an oriental rug need not lose its charm and beauty even when threadbare. It fades and wanes gracefully, it ages with dignity. The lovely pattern still shows, although the colours are more subdued. As long as a single knot remains, it is still – and everyone can see that it is – an oriental rug.

Many predict the disappearance of hand-knotted rugs in the course of this century. This is not likely to happen, for there is no need to suppose that mechanisation and industrialisation will be allowed to squeeze out the ancient handicraft with its wealth of tradition. But undoubtedly we have to expect that qualities will be coarser and prices dearer, and that many of the rugs finding their way to us in future will be marked by a certain uniformity.

Yet there is no cause for alarm; large stocks of genuine oriental rugs still exist. They are lying in Tehran and Copenhagen, in London and Stockholm and Leningrad, in Zürich and Hamburg, in Athens and Istanbul and in New York, and many another place. The rugs are waiting to be bought by those who wish to have constantly before them an example of the fine, ancient craft of the East, an oriental rug.

COLOUR-PLATES

1. Tabriz, Iran. 5′5″ x 7′10″ (1,65 x 2,40 m.)

2. Bijar, Iran. 4′4″ x 6′9″ (1,31 x 2,05 m.)

3. Ardabil, Iran. 3′4″ x 5′9″ (1,02 x 1,74 m.)

4. Mehriban, Iran. 4′11″ x 6′6″ (1,50 x 1,99 m.)

5. Hamadan, Iran. 4′6″ x 6′11″ (1,39 x 2,11 m.)

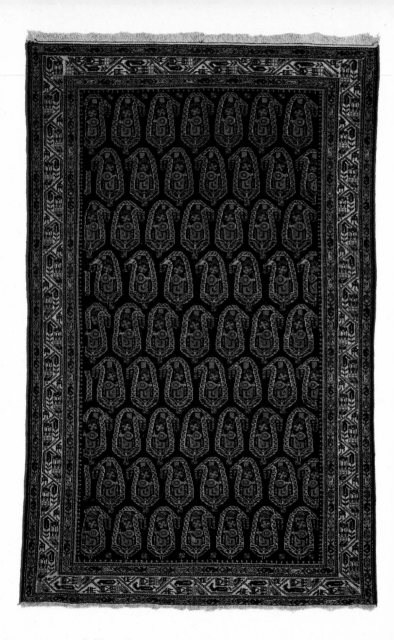

6. Hamadan, Iran. 4′5″ x 6′10″ (1,35 x 2,08 m.)

7. Mosul, Iran. 4′1″ x 6′3″ (1,25 x 1,91 m.)

8. Seraband, Iran. 4′1″ x 6′9″ (1,25 x 2,07 m.)

9. Saruck, Iran. 4′5″ x 6′9″ (1,34 x 2,07 m.)

10. Saruck, Iran. 3′5″ x 4′9″ (1,05 x 1,45 m.)

11. Senneh, Iran. 3′4″ x 5′ (1,02 x 1,53 m.)

12. Feraghan, Iran. 5′3″ x 10′7″ (1,60 x 3,23 m.) (cut)

13. Luristan, Iran. 4'1'' x 6'11'' (1,25 x 2,10 m.)

14. Kirman, Iran. 4'7'' x 7'3'' (1,40 x 2,21 m.)

15. Kirman, Iran. 4'6'' x 7'3'' (1,37 x 2,22 m.)

16. Qashgai, Iran. 5′7″ x 8′3″ (1,70 x 2,52 m.)

17. Afshar, Iran. 4′8″ x 6′3″ (1,41 x 1,90 m.)

18. Shiraz, Iran. 3′5″ x 4′11″ (1,05 x 1,51 m.)

19. Abadeh, Iran. 3′5″ x 5′ (1,05 x 1,54 m.)

20. Bakhtiari, Iran. 4'3" x 6'7" (1,30 x 2,00 m.)

21. Bakhtiari, Iran. 4′6″ x 7′4″ (1,37 x 2,23 m.)

22. Meshed, Iran. 5′2″ x 7′6″ (1,58 x 2,29 m.)

23. Nain, Iran. 4′9″ x 7′3″ (1,46 x 2,20 m.)

24. Kashan, Iran. 4′6″ x 7′2″ (1,36 x 2,18 m.)

25. Kashan, Iran. 4′6″ x 7′1″ (1,38 x 2,14 m.)

26. Qum, Iran. 4′3″ x 7′1″ (1,30 x 2,15 m.)

27. Qum, Iran. 4′6″ x 6′10″ (1,38 x 2,08 m.)

28. Joshaghan, Iran. 3′7″ x 5′2″ (1,10 x 1,58 m.)

29. Isfahan, Iran. 4′10″ x 7′6″ (1,49 x 2,30 m.)

30. Isfahan, Iran. 4′6″ x 6′6″ (1,37 x 2,00 m.)

31. Senneh Kelim, Iran. 3′11″ x 5′ (1,20 x 1,53 m.)

32. Azerbaijan Kelim, Iran. 3′11″ x 5′ (1,19 x 1,50 m.)

33. Shiraz Kelim, Iran. 5′6″ x 8′5″ (1,68 x 2,56 m.)

34. Kurdish Kelim, Iran. 5′4″ x 9′11″ (1,63 x 3,03 m.)

35. Yomud, Turkoman. 3′1″ x 4′10″ (0,95 x 1,47 m.)

36. Tekke, Turkoman. 4'1'' x 5'3'' (1,26 x 1,61 m.)

37. Early Salor, Turkoman. 4′6″ x 6′ (1,38 x 1,85 m.)

38. Beshir Juval, Turkoman. 3′2″ x 5′6″ (0,98 x 1,67 m.)

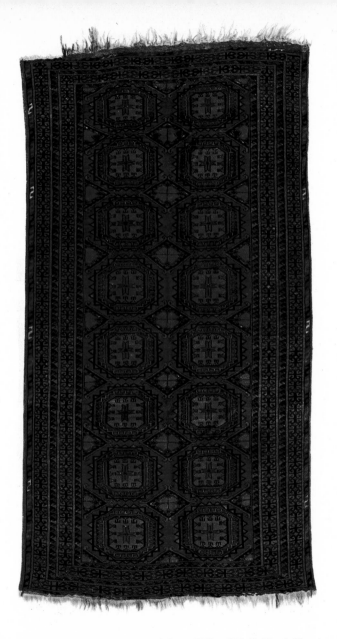

39. Early Afghan, Afghanistan. 3′7″ x 6′5″ (1,09 x 1,95 m.)

40. Afghan, Afghanistan. 4′10″ x 6′1″ (1,50 x 1,87 m.)

41. Kachli, Afghanistan. 5'6" x 7'1" (1,69 x 2,15 m.)

42. Baluchi, N.E. Iran. 4′ x 7′11″ (1,23 x 2,15 m.)

43. Baluchi, N.E. Iran. 3′5″ x 6′4″ (1,05 x 1,93 m.)

44. Baluchi, N.E. Iran. 3′2″ x 6′ (0,97 x 1,85 m.)

45. Baluchi Runner, N.E. Iran. 3′8″ x 12′6″ (1,12 x 3,81 m.) (cut)

46a. Qashgai Pouch, Iran. 2′3″ x 4′ (0,69 x 1,21 m.)

46b. Baluchi Torba, N.E. Iran. 1′5″ x 2′7″ (0,44 x 0,80 m.)

47. Derbend, Caucasus. 4′5″ x 6′5″ (1,35 x 1,95 m.)

48. Early Kuba, Caucasus. 4′8″ x 8′3″ (1,42 x 2,52 m.)

49. Early Kazak, Caucasus. 4′6″ x 6′10″ (1,37 x 2,08 m.)

50. Early Shirvan, Caucasus. 4′1″ x 7′11″ (1,26 x 2,15 m.)

51. Early Shirvan, Caucasus. 4'2" x 6' (1,28 x 1,82 m.)

52. Shirvan, Caucasus. 3'8" x 5'8" (1,12 x 1,73 m.)

53. Shirvan, Caucasus. 3′2″ x 6′7″ (0,98 x 2,00 m.)

54. Mudjur Prayer-Rug, Turkey. 3′4″ x 4′10″ (1,02 x 1,48 m.)

55. Kula, Turkey. 3′4″ x 6′3″ (1,03 x 1,90 m.)

56. Anatolian Runner, Turkey. 3'10" x 10'4" (1,17 x 3,15 m.) (cut)

57. Ladik, Turkey. 3′9″ x 5′3″ (1,15 x 1,60 m.)

58. Silk Saph, Turkey. 2′7″ x 7′9″ (0,80 x 2,38 m.)

59. Turkoman Design, Pakistan. 4′2″ x 5′11″ (1,29 x 1,80 m.)

60. Caucasian Design, Pakistan. 4′5″ x 6′6″ (1,35 x 1,97 m.)

61. Panjde Design, Pakistan. 4′5″ x 6′6″ (1,35 x 1,97 m.)

62. Early Chinese Rug. 5′11″ x 8′6″ (1,80 x 2,60 m.)

63. Early Chinese Cock Rug. 4'5" x 6'9" (1,34 x 2,05 m.)

64. Chinese Rug. 3′1″ x 5′4″ (0,95 x 1,64 m.)

RUGS IN DETAIL

The rugs illustrated and described in this book may be generally regarded as the types most commonly seen on the market today.

On the colour-plates the length of the rugs is given exclusive of fringe, but inclusive of borders, if any. The width is always measured at the narrowest point.

In the description below, the numbers at the head of each section correspond to the numbers on the plates.

1. Tabriz, Iran

Tabriz, the town where this rug was made, is today one of the chief centres of rug-making. It lies in the north-west of Iran, of which it was once the capital, and a large rug-trade is still carried on in the bazaars.

Rugs are made in all sizes. Warp and weft are of cotton. The pile is wool of a good quality. Both Senneh and Ghiordes knots are used. The density of the knots ranges from coarse to very compact. The pile often feels slightly hard, because the water used by Tabriz rug-dyers contains a lot of salt.

In this rug the ground is cream, but rugs with a red or blue ground also occur.

Many Tabriz rugs, like the one in the illustration, have animal or hunting patterns; medallion and floral patterns are also very characteristic. The borders are always beautifully designed.

Tabriz is also the depot for fine runners, Kellegis, and rugs from other parts of north-west Iran, such as Heriz, Sarab and Karaj.

2. Bijar, Iran

This rug was made by Kurds, and is definitely one of the strongest types of rug now obtainable in Iran. The knot is Senneh. Bijar rugs are always very firmly and closely knotted, and, therefore, extremely hard-wearing. Strong hand-spun wool is used for the pile. Warp and weft may be either cotton or wollen, but are usually cotton. It is a rug rich in tradition, drawing extensively on historic patterns. The rug illustrated is typical, with a central area enclosed by the small, repeating Herati pattern. The central field is framed in strong lines with stepped ends. The colours are red and blue. The pattern is multi-coloured. Bijar rugs have a wide main border, and usually three to eight smaller borders. Rugs are made in many sizes, including very large ones.

3. Ardabil, Iran

To many the name Ardabil suggests the *sacred carpets,* also known as the Ardabil carpets (see p. 10), in the Victoria and Albert Museum, and the Los Angeles Country Museum of Art.

The example in this book was made in the north of Iran, in the country round Ardabil, wich lies not far from the frontiers of the Soviet Union. The warp is wool, but in these rugs may also be cotton. Weft and pile are also woollen. The ground may be blue or cream-coloured as well as red. The pattern is usually rather stylised, often resembling those of Caucasian rugs, though the figures are not rendered quite so geometrically.

Generally we find medallions and squares with the stylised flowers, mentioned earlier, making an attractive contrast to the quiet ground. In this rug the knotting is usually firm and regular, and it may be recommended as a good and useful type.

4. Mehriban, Iran

The Mehriban rug, as well as the three described above, comes from the Azerbaijan group in northern Iran. It is, like the Heriz and Goravan rugs, rather coarsely knotted, always on cotton, with pile of rather a coarse wool. The design is made up of highly stylised flowers, geometrical medallions and corner-patterns.

The one illustrated is a typical Mehriban in bold, one might say harsh, colouring, with red as the chief colour, and blue and beige also used. The pattern of this particular rug is sometimes called a Heriz pattern.

5. Hamadan, Iran

The Hamadan rug is often and rightly praised as a good, solid rug. It is made in the large district of western Iran where the town of Hamadan serves as a depot for more than a thousand villages. This is one reason for the wide variations of design found in the rugs known as Hamadan. The Hamadan rug is knotted on a foundation of cotton (though the weft-threads are sometimes woollen), and the pile is of strong wool. The Ghiordes knot is employed. In our example the colour of the ground is camel-hair brown, a favoured choice in Hamadan rugs. The other colours are generally a subdued red and blue, more rarely green. The medallion

seen on the rug is typical of the Hamadan district.

6. Hamadan, Iran

This is another rug from the large Hamadan district. The foundation is cotton, the pile is wool of a soft quality. The borders harmoniously enclose a large central field covered with the pine or cone pattern *Mir-i-bota*, which is beautifully set on the plain ground.

Hamadan rugs are mostly found in rather small sizes, many of them being the work of nomads (see p. 15).

7. Mosul, Iran

The Mosul rug is a typical example of a rug from the Hamadan district. It was, however, not made in the town of Hamadan, which has been a rug-centre for several hundred years, but, like the rugs known as Borchelu, Bubukabad, Maslaghan and Saveh, comes from the surrounding country. The one in the picture is knotted on a foundation of cotton. The wool used for the pile is coarse, and the knotting not very dense. The colours can be extremely varied, and there may be great variations in quality in the rugs from this large area.

8. Seraband, Iran

Made in the town of Seraband, in the west of Iran. The rug is knotted on a foundation of cotton, and the pile is wool. The knot employed is usually Senneh, though the Ghiordes knot can also be found. The ground is generally red, but in rare cases may be blue. The design (frequently copied in machine-made rugs) is a pine-pattern repeated throughout the rug. This pattern, also called *Mir-i-bota* (see ill. p.

Dogtooth border and key pattern

26), is arranged in rows, often so as to face alternately right and left. The large central field is framed in attractive borders, made up of a main border and several lesser borders. The smaller ones match one another (see ill.).

Seraband rugs are usually knotted firmly, but coarsely, and because of their thick pile lie well on the floor. They are strong and thus hard-wearing. A particularly handsome rug of the same design is the Mir rug. It often has a smaller pattern, the borders are more numerous, the knotting is more regular and firm, and the wool better-looking and more lustrous. It is, therefore, also a more expensive rug.

9. Saruck, Iran

The town of Saruck situated south-west of Tehran, the capital, produces a rug of the same name. Saruck rugs are usually made of handsome, lustrous wool; the knotting is dense, firm and regular. The knot is Senneh, and the foundation cotton, which gives a very stout rug. In fact Saruck rugs are amongst the most hard-wearing Persian rugs. The ground is red or blue, very occasionally cream. Usually the

design is richly ornamented, often reminding one of a Kirman or Kashan rug. This example is a pleasing, harmonious composition with a central medallion, corner-patterns, and a fine, ornamented border.

10. Saruck, Iran

This rug comes from the same district at the previous one, though the composition, showing American influence, is a little different. Here again we have a central area and delicate flower-sprays. The colour is copper, and the rug both strongly and closely knotted. Like most Saruck rugs, this one lies firmly and well on the floor.

11. Senneh, Iran

This rug is made near the town of Senneh in the west of Iran. Generally it has a foundation of cotton, but there may be wool in the weft. The pile is wool. Oddly enough the knot is usually Ghiordes, (due to the fact that most of the inhabitants are of Turkish descent), but one can also find rugs from Senneh with the Senneh knot.

No. 11 is a typical Senneh rug, with its blue ground and angular design. Rugs from the Senneh district often have the pine or another smallish pattern repeated over the whole rug, which is seldom large. Senneh rugs have character, and are softer than, for instance, Kashan rugs. The back of Senneh rugs is rough as there is only one shoot of the weft between each row of knots, and this forces the warp threads back alternately.

12. Feraghan, Iran

A beautiful, semi-antique Feraghan runner from the famous district in the west of Iran, one of the biggest rug-exporting areas in the country. Feraghan rugs are knotted on a foundation of cotton, with a woollen pile. Both Ghiordes and Senneh knots are used. The Herati, or Feraghan, pattern of the rug in this illustration is typical of the district.

Herati or Feraghan pattern

This pattern occurs in various sizes and degrees of elaboration. The colours are reddish or dark blue, possibly with a greenish border. This rug is widely used in the western world. It should be added that many of the coarser rugs from the Feraghan district are marketed in Europe and America under the name of *Mahal*.

13. Luristan, Iran

The Luri, or Luristan, rugs are made by nomads in the rather inaccessible parts of western Iran south of Kurdistan. The foundation is usually wool or cattle-hair, but they may also have a cotton warp and a woollen weft. The pile is wool, and the knots are Ghiordes. These rugs usually show a strong

geometrical influence. No. 13 has three diamonds on a very dark blue and characteristic ground. Dark colours are common. The pile is fairly deep, and the wool coarse, but of very good quality.

14. Kirman, Iran

The large town of Kirman in the south of Iran produces handsome and lustrous drawing room carpets in dense and strong qualities and many sizes, right up to $11'6'' \times 16'6''$ ($3,50 \times 5,00$ m.). The foundation is cotton, the pile fine wool, and the knots Senneh. Pastel shades often appear in the ground of these rugs, for instance, a pale cream, green or blue. The design is very conservative, and old traditions have been continued in their floral patterns, especially in the stylised roses.

15. Kirman, Iran

This is a typical Kirman rug, with a beautifully designed centre medallion set off by the plain blue ground. The rug is enclosed in a broken floral border, thus exemplifying the Iranian combination of patterns. Such richly decorated rugs with flowers and flower-sprays scattered over the whole field are very popular in England, and have for many years been produced specially for the English market.

Of course, not all the rug-making is done in Kirman itself; rugs are made in the surrounding country as well, but nearly all of them are marketed under the name of Kirman. An exception are rugs from the towns of Yezd and Raver situated north and south of Kirman. They are usually described as 'Kirman Yezd' and 'Kirman Raver'. It is not unusual to find people or animals in Kirman rugs.

16. Qashgai, Iran

The Qashgais are one of the largest nomadic tribes of Iran, living in the wide area north-west of Shiraz. Qashgai rugs are generally made by women. The rugs have a foundation of wool, possibly mixed with cattle-hair; the pile is wool of an excellent quality. The knotting is Senneh, though rugs with the Ghiordes knot can also be found. The usual colours are red, reddish-brown, blue and cream. The centre is often diamond shaped. The ground of the Qashgai rug is covered with small geometrical figures very skilfully arranged. There may be dogs and birds, petals and rosettes, stars and crosses.

17. Afshar, Iran

The Afshar rug is made by nomads or semi-nomads living in the area between Shiraz and Kirman. Their original home was between the Euphrates and the Tigris, but they quarrelled with the Turkish sultan on a question of taxes, and *Shah Abbas the Great* (1586–1628, see p. 26) agreed to receive them into Persia, where they have been ever since. Though made by nomads, these rugs often have a foundation of cotton, since the Afshars take them to Kirman for sale and get cotton in exchange. The pile is wool, and the knots Ghiordes, though some instances of the Senneh knot may be found. The design is often composed of diamonds with stylised flowers covering the whole central field. The colours are varied, but the ground is usually red or blue. White or cream-coloured wool is another feature of the Afshar rug.

18. Shiraz, Iran

This rug, like the previous two, is the work of nomads, and so is fairly soft. It is knotted on a foundation of wool and cattle-hair, with a woollen pile. These rugs are made by Qashgai tribes (see no. 16), and many of them are collected for transport in the town of Shiraz, in southern Iran. Shiraz rugs are generally more loosely knotted than, for example, Qashgai rugs. The colours of the ground are red and blue, more rarely cream, and often crude and rather harsh. The design has usually a stepped diamond outline which encloses a number of stylised, geometrical animal and flower patterns. In rugs from this district the edges are often bound with different colours of worsted, and also it is not unusual to find little tassels adorning them.

19. Abadeh, Iran

In southern Iran, on the road from Shiraz to Isfahan, lies the town of Abadeh, where the rugs of that name are made. Their foundation is cotton, the pile is wool, and their knots Senneh. The colouring is generally harmonious; red, terracotta, brown and blue are used, and to a lesser extent, green. The designs, though very like those of Qashgai rugs, are essentially a mixture of Iranian and Caucasian rug-designs. A central medallion is placed in a diamond shaped field with a red ground. Similar medallions often appear in the corners of the rug with a green ground. Small flower and leaf patterns are scattered imaginatively all over the rug, which is framed by narrow borders.

20. Bakhtiari, Iran

The nomadic tribes of the Bakhtiari live in the south of Iran, between Isfahan and the Persian Gulf. Originally they came from Turkey. Their rugs, knotted on a foundation of cotton with a good, strong wool as pile, are in general evenly made, and extremely hard-wearing. The knots are Ghiordes. The colours are often very bold with shades of red, rust, blue and cream predominating. The design is frequently divided into small compartments covering the whole centre of the rug, each of which contains stylised floral decorations. In no. 20 the field has a stylised 'tree of life' in the middle, around which the other stylised floral ornaments are arranged.

21. Bakhtiari, Iran

All the different villages in the Bakhtiari region have their special designs. No. 21 is a typical Bakhtiari rug, here with a centre medallion. Bakhtiari rugs are usually made of rather dry wool. Another characteristic feature is that the weft-threads, which are blue, tend to show very distinctly at the back. It is not unusual for a Bakhtiari rug of superior quality to be described as a *Bibibaff* rug. That simply means that it was made by women; *bibi* is the Iranian word for 'woman', and *baff* for 'knot'.

22. Meshed, Iran

Near the Turkestan border of eastern Iran, in the big territory named Khurasan, is the town of Meshed, important as a collecting-centre for rugs which for that reason are often given the same name. Meshed is also a depot for some nomad rugs.

Meshed rugs are knotted on a foundation of cotton, though in some cases there may be wool in the weft. The pile is wool, not usually very good in quality, since it is apt to be too soft. Red is the most usual colour, but the ground may be mauve, with a pattern in cream. Meshed rugs often have a well-designed centre medallion, like the one in the illustration, and large corner-patterns. The ground of the rug is strewn with an abundance of multi-coloured posies and leaves. The whole rug has a frame of borders, made up, in the best Iranian tradition, of a broad main border and several lesser borders.

The *Turkbaff* rugs come from the same area. These rugs are made by Turkish-speaking weavers, hence the name 'Turkish knot'. The Ghiordes knot produces a slightly granulated back; the colours are frequently the same as in Meshed rug. A star with many rays is often used as a centre medallion.

23. Nain, Iran

In the centre of Iran lies the town of Nain which has given its name to local rugs. Nain rugs usually have Senneh knots, a foundation of cotton, and a pile of wool of a handsome and exquisite quality. Nain rugs are generally very finely and regularly knotted, and are some of the most distinguished rugs made in Iran. The ground is often red or cream, and the design with its beautiful, harmonious decoration is typical of the workshop-made Iranian rug.

The Nain rug shown here is composed of a skilfully designed central medallion, and fine corner-patterns, with lotus-flowers in the central field which is, of course, framed by main borders and several lesser borders. The effect is attractive and well-balanced.

24. Kashan, Iran

This rug comes from a very important district of Iran, producing rugs of exceptional density and firmness. Many fine rugs were made here in the sixteenth century, which is known as Persia's golden age. It was only about a hundred years ago, after a lapse of several centuries, that these excellent, hard-wearing rugs again came to be made in any number. The Kashan rug is knotted on a foundation of cotton; the pile is fine, and of excellent wool. The ground is usually red or blue, the design varied in colour. No. 24 is a typical Kashan rug, with a medallion in the middle, corner-patterns, and a ground covered with elegant sprays of leaves and flowers, beautifully and subtly connected. The borders are blue, and like the central field contain lotus-flowers.

25. Kashan, Iran

This is an example of the vase Kashan or 'Hadgi Nanoumi pattern', as it is called, on a blue ground and with a profusion of colours in the design. A number of the finest Iranian rugs come from this locality, where the rich traditions of Iranian design are carried on with incredible industry and exactness. One may also find Kashan rugs displaying columns or a fine Iranian house. Silk rugs occur in which both foundation and pile are silk. In Iran these silk Kashans are never used on the floor, but only on walls.

26. Qum, Iran

South of the Iranian capital lies the town of Qum, one of the oldest in the country. Here *Shah Abbas* (see p. 26) is buried. The Qum rug is usually knotted on a foundation of cotton, though the weft may be wool. Generally it has a firm dense woollen pile made with Senneh knots, and trimmed closely and evenly. The colours of the ground are cream and dark or light blue, seldom red. The design is often multi-coloured. The illustration shows a medallion rug with birds on a cream ground.

27. Qum, Iran

This Qum rug, like no. 26, is densely and evenly knotted. Rugs from Qum (which are not produced in great numbers) are usually easy to recognise because of their delicate pastel shades. The one illustrated is a golden cream-colour, with the *Mir-i bota* pine pattern (see p. 26) so popular in the East. This pattern is repeated not only in rows throughout the whole central field but also in the main border. The designs of modern Qum rugs are sometimes copied from old ones in museums or private collections.

28. Joshaghan, Iran

In central Iran, slightly north of Isfahan, lies the town of Joshaghan, which in the eighteenth and early nineteenth century produced some very handsome and densely knotted rugs. These rugs had a central field of rosettes linked by flower-sprays.

The rugs which are now sold under the name of Joshaghan are rather different in appearance. The one in the illustration has a foundation of cotton and a woollen pile with Senneh knots. The design, which is being copied in the workshops of Kashan and Tabriz, is many-coloured, and cleverly divided into a lattice of diamonds. Each diamond is formed by a stylised flower or spray. There is often a large diamond-shaped medallion in the middle of Joshaghan rugs, and the pattern stands out very clearly. The wool is excellent, and the rug, which is rather coarsely knotted, is hard-wearing.

29. Isfahan, Iran

Shah Abbas (see p. 26) the great patron of building and art, founded the famous workshops of Isfahan, which at the same time he made his capital. For centuries Isfahan rugs have been treasured both in the East and in Europe. They are still, in general, beautifully worked; densely and firmly knotted on a foundation of cotton, sometimes with a wollen weft. The knots are Senneh, and the ground is mostly red or beige. The design is usually many-coloured. The rug shown here is a beautiful example of a fine, very closely knotted Isfahan, made not long ago, and with more than 800 knots to the square inch. Of course the price of such a fine rug is high. It has an elegant small central medallion, together with the winding sprays and skilful corner design so typical of Isfahan rugs. The central field is framed by a wide main border of Shah Abbas patterns and lotus-flowers, with matching narrow borders. The woven inscription reads (from right to left): 'Serafian, Isfahan, Iran'.

30. Isfahan, Iran

This brand-new Isfahan rug might well be a product of the art school in Tehran, where new designs are being worked out all the time. In this case the design is faithful to Isfahan traditions; it has a central

medallion, winding sprays on a reddish ground, and a beige main border. The pattern is rather more crude, and the knotting nothing like so dense, regular and exact as in no. 29, nor are the colours so well chosen; but it is undoubtedly typical of some recent works.

Animal patterns still occur in Isfahan rugs.

31. Senneh Kelim, Iran

Senneh Kelim rugs often have a characteristic diamond-shaped central area, surrounded by intertwining and highly stylised flower-sprays. The usual colours are blue or red, mixed with a little orange, brown and green.

32. Azerbaijan Kelim, Iran

The design is not so blurred in these rugs as in Senneh Kelims, and the colours are purer. This rug has two small birds like geese woven into the central area.

33. Shiraz Kelim, Iran

The wandering Qashgai tribes also make kelims, of which no. 33 is a typical example, with the two diamond-shaped motifs taking up the whole of the rug, and creating a strong effect of zigzag striping. The zigzag stripes, although bold in colour, are a fine and tasteful combination of blue, red and green. Note the small, decorative star-like figures woven into two of the corners, and into the triangles halfway up the rug.

34. Kurdish Kelim, Iran

Some of the most beautiful kelims are woven by Kurds living in western Iran, on the Iraqi border. This kelim has a very dark ground, and the central field is filled with octagonal panels, containing stars and rosettes. In these octagons the colours are used diagonally. The large central field is framed by a number of matching borders (see ill. p. 115).

35. Yomud, Turkoman

These rugs, which are well thought of, come from the large area between North Iran, the Caspian Sea, Uzbekistan and Afghanistan, and are made by Yomuds, a nomadic Turkoman tribe. Like the other rugs from this area they are knotted on a foundation of wool, sometimes mixed with cattle-hair. The pile is also wool. As a rule the knotting is Senneh, and usually even and dense.

The pile of Turkoman rugs is generally clipped very closely. The chief colour in these rugs is red but it may vary greatly in shade from a light red to a deep crimson which is nearly purple. The selvages of Yomud rugs are often oversown with red or blue wool. The octagon or 'gul' is typical, and it is placed in straight lines up and across the rug.

36. Tekke, Turkoman

The Tekke tribe is the largest in Turkmenistan; it is believed to have 200,000 members. They are semi-nomads who live in the country round Ashkhabad and Merv, where the best rugs are made. The foundation is wool, and so is the pile. The knotting is Senneh. It should be mentioned that the knotting is usually denser and if possible even more accurate, than in Yomud rugs. The Tekke tribe has very diligent rug-weavers, and a large proportion of the rugs known as 'Turkoman rugs' are their work. The sizes produced are often

adapted to European conditions, and carpets as large as 4×5 yards are made occasionally.

The Tekke weavers also fill in the space between the octagons with tarantula patterns or with stylised stars or hooks. This type of rug has been sold to Europe on a large scale. The colours are attractive and warm, and the designs fit easily into any kind of interior, whether modern or old-fashioned. The red ground-colour is often lighter in shade than that of Yomud rugs. Kachli-rugs (see plate 41) for tent doors are fairly common.

37. Early Salor, Turkoman

A handsome, well designed rug with two rows of octagons, leaving room for a fair-sized tarantula pattern. The rug is technically similar to nos. 35 and 36. This example has an interesting feature; there are white, brown and black animals in the main border. The ground of Salor rugs is usually some shade of red, from reddish brown to copper, though an occasional example may have a cream or green ground.

38. Beshir Juval, Turkoman

Beshir rugs are made near the river Amu Darya (Oxus), in the country round Beshir, which lies about 125 miles south of Bokhara. They are similar in general terms to other Turkoman rugs, but foreign influences can often be detected in their patterns. The foundation is wool, frequently mixed with cattle-hair. The pile is wool, the knotting Senneh. The principal colour is red, but there are often bluish and yellowish patterns; green may also appear in the design.

The 'cloud-band' is a pattern which is frequently seen in Beshir rugs. The rug in the illustration has another typical Beshir design; a field covered with patterns on a terracotta ground. The motifs are stylised stars, rosettes and leaves. The pure yellow is most effective.

No. 38 is a Juval with a knotted front and a plain woven back. The owner can store his possessions in this bag both in his tent, and when travelling on his camel. It is made by the women of the tribe, not for export but for their own use. Juvals are also made by the other Turkoman and Afghan tribes.

39. Early Afghan, Afghanistan

Afghan rugs have been in great demand for some years, probably owing to the warm red colouring, the simple pattern, the fairly deep and strong pile, and last but not least, the moderate price; it is usual to get value for money, whether buying an unwashed or a lustrous, washed Afghan rug.

Kabul, the capital of Afghanistan, is an important depot. Many rugs are also collected in the town of Herat. The foundation is wool, sometimes mixed with cattle-hair. The pile is woollen, and the knotting usually Senneh. The colour of the old rug in the illustration is copper. The design is carried out in shades of very dark blue, almost black.

40. Afghan, Afghanistan

A typical modern Afghan rug, knotted on a foundation of wool and cattle-hair. The pile is wool, and the knotting Senneh. The colour a beautiful red, the wool lustrous. The octagons or 'gul' are a very dark blue, verging on black; in some rugs they are a very dark green.

The 'guls', placed in rows and nearly touching each other vertically, tend to be a great deal bigger than in Yomud and Tekke rugs. The design of the 'gul', which has a quartering of two light and two dark patches, is filled with a pattern like a clover-leaf. It is quite common to find Afghan rugs with white patterns in the octagons and borders. The quality varies a great deal, especially the evenness of the knotting.

Some modern Afghan rugs very closely resemble Turkoman rugs (see p. 27) in design, colour and quality. These are woven by nomadic Turkoman tribes now settled in Afghanistan.

41. Kachli, Afghanistan

The technical characteristics, including the red ground, are the same as in Afghan rugs (nos. 39 and 40). This is the rug that forms the opening of the tent. It has a cross-like design dividing the rug into four parts, often with patterns resembling candlesticks. It was once assumed that rugs with the cross design had been made by Christian weavers, but that is not the case. The figure has nothing to do with the Christian cross. The same pattern occurs in a number of Turkoman rugs. In some cases the rug has two straps at the top by which to hang it.

42. Baluchi, N.E. Iran

The Baluchi tribes are nomads, living with their sheep and goats in the country round Meshed, and southwards towards the Persian Gulf. Occasionally they may cross a frontier, for such things are not taken very seriously. Their chief concern is to find good pastures for their flocks.

No. 42 is an ordinary Baluchi rug of quite good quality, knotted on a foundation of wool an cattle-hair, and with the Senneh knot. The usual colours are red and sometimes brown with blue and a little white. The designs are geometrical, but often more imaginative than those of Afghan rugs.

43. Baluchi, N.E. Iran

Another typical Baluchi rug, geometrical in design, with red as the predominant colour, but with touches of blue and white. The design shows considerable imagination and the effect is rich and yet subtle. The ground is sprinkled with stylised stars and rosettes.

Baluchi rugs are usually rather small, and very suitable with contemporary furnishings.

There is a distinction between the Baluchi rugs brought into Meshed, and often described in the trade as 'Meshed-Baluchis', and the rugs despatched to overseas markets via Karachi. The quality of the former is very much better than that of the latter.

44. Baluchi, N.E. Iran

A prayer-rug with the mihrab or 'prayer-niche'. A motif like the palm of a hand is woven at the top of the rug on either side of the mihrab. The central field is occupied by pine or leaf-patterns. The figures are arranged in rows facing alternately right and left, and the rug is framed by a broad main border and several lesser borders. The colouring is typical of Baluchi rugs; dark brown with a golden tinge, mixed with red, dark blue and a little white.

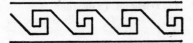

'Running dog' border

In these rugs the foundation is generally wool, often mixed with cattle-hair; the pile is wool, knotted with the Senneh knot. This type of rug is usually reasonable in price and very well suited to a modern house.

45. Baluchi Runner, N.E. Iran

Baluchi runners are uncommon, and usually rather small, about 4'1" × 13' (1,25 × 4,00 m.). One may, however, see them in carpet sizes of about 7'6" × 13' (2,30 × 4,00 m.), but that is rare.

Baluchi runner no. 45 is technically the same as nos. 43 and 44.

46a. Qashgai Pouch, Iran

This is a saddle-bag, made by Qashgai nomads. The knot and the other technical details are the same as in no. 16. This type of saddle-bag is used by the nomads to carry their possessions when travelling. They sling it across the neck of a horse or mule.

46b. Baluchi Torba, N.E. Iran

This type of bag, known as a *torba*, is used for storing personal possessions, but also sometimes as a cushion stuffed with feathers.

They are not normally made for export, but for domestic use; that is the reason why they are often carefully and beautifully made, and they can be very decorative. No. 46b is made by the usual Baluchi methods (see p. 30).

47. Derbend, Caucasus

The town of Derbend is situated on the Caspian Sea in the eastern part of the mountainous region of Daghestan. It is from this town that the rug takes its name. It is a firmly and densely knotted rug of excellent quality. The foundation and the pile are woollen, and the rug is knotted with the Ghiordes knot. In rugs from this area the ground is usually red or blue, and the geometrical design many-coloured.

The one illustrated is a typical Derbend, since one, two or three medallions often occur in the central field. These medallions are roughly square, their decoration radiating from the centre. The border around the central field is highly stylised. The rug shown is an early example, but the women of Derbend still make rugs which are as good in quality as the old ones. However, in modern rugs the foundation is cotton and the designs rather simplified.

48. Early Kuba, Caucasus

The town of Kuba is situated south of Derbend (see no. 47). Kuba and the surrounding country are populated by descendants of the Turks. Here, as in other parts of the Caucasus, the manufacture of rugs has been carefully organised.

A typical old Kuba rug with a severely geometrical pattern and dense, even pile is very rare. The Kuba rug illustrated has a foundation and pile of wool. The

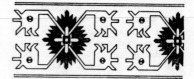

Crab border

knotting is Ghiordes. The colouring is characteristic, and so is the broad border with the S-shaped patterns. The quality of these rugs is considered to be one of the highest in the Caucasus. It is a rug for connoisseurs, and old Russian rugs are not cheap. In Kuba, as in Derbend, hand-knotted rugs are still being made, but they lack the charm of the early ones.

49. Early Kazak, Caucasus

Kazak rugs were, and still are, made in Trans-Caucasia by the Turks of Azerbaijan. They often display two or three geometrical medallions with characteristic S-shaped patterns. The 'crab' border of linked rosettes seen in this rug is also typical. The foundation is usually wool, and the fairly deep pile is always wool, with the Ghiordes knot. The principal colour is red, though bold, warm shades of green and yellow are used as well. The type illustrated is also known as a 'cloudband Kazak' because of the devices in the medallions. Another characteristic Kazak pattern shows a vague resemblance to the old crest of Imperial Russia, the double eagle.

Kazak rugs have always been popular in Europe, largely because of their robust quality. Kazak rugs were once, wrongly, believed to be made by the Cossacks. Today, output is negligible.

S-border

50. Early Shirvan, Caucasus

The Shirvan rugs come from the plains along the banks of the river Kura, and are surely the best known and most widely distributed of Caucasian rugs. Early Shirvans can be had occasionally, but prices are high. They are knotted on a wollen and cotton warp, often a twist of one brown and one white thread. Both weft and pile are wool, and the Ghiordes knot is used. The knotting is dense and regular, but the wool not quite so lustrous as in other Caucasian rugs. In early rugs, blue is often the dominant colour, but red and cream are also used. The design is many-coloured and geometrical. The illustration shows a typical early Shirvan, with a blue ground and a decidedly geometrical, star-like pattern.

51. Early Shirvan, Caucasus

The technical details resemble no. 50. The colours are bright and pure. The ground of the rug is covered by various stars and rosettes, and the central field framed in a main border and several narrow borders. Birds rather like swans, and a pattern like a ram's horn are often found in the Shirvan rugs (see drawing). The size does not exceed 5' × 11'6" (1,50 × 3,50 m.)

Ram's horn pattern

52. Shirvan, Caucasus

'Shirvan' (nos. 52 and 53) is becoming a generic term for the new, modern product; all the variations which appear in early Caucasian rugs from, say, the Derbend, Kuba and Kazak districts have almost disappeared.

Current production is directed and controlled by the government, and is of good quality. The knotting is dense and even, the pile strong. The rug is undoubtedly hard-wearing. The illustration shows one of the new Shirvan rugs. It is knotted on a foundation of cotton with a woollen pile, and a Ghiordes knot. The design is geometrical, with horns and swans (see text to no. 51).

53. Shirvan, Caucasus

Another example of a new Shirvan, produced like most of the new Caucasian rugs, under state monopoly. The weaver is furnished with dyed yarn, excellently spun, and other materials, sometimes including a loom. Accounts are settled when she delivers the finished rug. State representatives also undertake the sale of the rugs.

The technical details of the rug illustrated in no. 53 are the same as for no. 52. Note the 'wineglass border'. This rug is of good quality, but perhaps it is noticeable that the personal touch is missing.

54. Mudjur Prayer-Rug, Turkey

This rug comes from the town of Mudjur in central Turkey. It is also known as a *Namaslyk*, the Turkish word for prayer-rug.

The Mudjur rug is knotted on a foundation of wool. The pile is also wool, and the knotting Ghiordes.

Wineglass border

The ground is usually red, in rare cases blue or cream. There are always several borders. The actual prayer-field is red, though blue or green niches may also be found. Some Mudjur have a stylised 'tree of life' in the field. The mihrab has a stepped outline.

The rug in the illustration (which is also shown on the cover of the book) is an early Mudjur, and is, incidentally, quite similar to a Ghiordes rug, though the latter usually has columns as part of the pattern. As in most Anatolian rugs, the colouring is bold, and the knotting fairly coarse. These Namaslyks are becoming rare.

55. Kula, Turkey

Rugs are still made in Turkey, but at present not many are exported. The rug shown is modern. It has a rather coarse wollen pile tied with Ghiordes knots on a foundation of wool. The knotting is not very firm, and this seems a soft rug, partly because of the woollen foundation; but the pile is deep, so that it is hard-wearing. The ground is red, though cream grounds are also found. The design is many-coloured, and bold in tone. The rug has an angular medallion in a diamond shaped field with stepped ends. It was obviously woven for export, since the words of the inscription 'Ali Ak 1954' have been written in Roman letters. This type of rug is quite common.

56. Anatolian Runner, Turkey

The name 'Anatolian' is used when the origin of the rug cannot be precisely located.

This runner is knotted on a foundation of wool; the pile is deep and of good quality. It is brightly coloured in red, dark, blue, gold and cream. On close inspection a row of towers, minarets and palms can be seen in the main border. This is a modern, but well-made rug.

57. Ladik, Turkey

Ladik, in the south of Turkey, used to be famous for its handsome prayer-rugs. For several centuries the town was large and flourishing, but now little of the ancient splendour remains.

Ladik rugs are knotted with the Ghiordes knot on a foundation of wool. The ground is red, though blue also occurs; green is rare. In early rugs, now mostly confined to museums, the colours are very subtle, while in modern rugs the colouring tends to be crude. The design is framed in a main border and several narrow secondary borders. The mihrab is obtuse and stepped. The Ladik rug is easily identified because tulips, usually an odd number, are woven into the rug beneath the prayer-field. The early rug in the illustration, though rather loosely knotted, is well preserved; the colour scheme is unusual.

58. Silk Saph, Turkey

This rug is called a family prayer-rug, and has nine prayer-niches. The earliest of these rugs are believed to have been made in Oushak about the beginning of the seventeenth century. Today, a limited number are made in Turkey for export. These rugs are eminently suitable as wall-decoration.

The example illustrated is knotted on a foundation of cotton, and the pile is spun silk. Some rugs of this type are made entirely of silk, but the price is then very high. The number of prayer-niches may vary from five to nine, and at least one of them is ivory-coloured; the others are gold, blue, red and green. A border encloses the niches, binding the design together.

59. Turkoman Design, Pakistan

Since 1948 there has been a considerable rug-making industry in Pakistan, centred in the towns of Karachi, Lahore and Hyderabad. The industry tries to produce rugs of good quality, and zealously copies designs from other rug-making areas. The designs adopted are more often Turkoman or Caucasian than Iranian.

No. 59 is an example of a so-called Bokhara rug with a light ground, knotted on a foundation of wool with a woollen pile. The knotting is Senneh; it is dense and very even, but the pile is rather too soft.

60. Caucasian Design, Pakistan

A Pakistani rug from Karachi, but with a Caucasian-inspired design. This is severely geometrical, with three star-shaped medallions, a broad 'wineglass border', and several lesser borders. The foundation is wool, and the rug has a close even pile made with Senneh knots, but is rather soft.

61. Panjde Design, Pakistan

In years to come more and more Pakistani rugs will probably find their way to Europe and America. The illustration shows a particularly handsome rug with a Turkoman Salor-Panjde design, made in Pakistan. (Members of the Salor tribe living in the Panjde oasis usually make rugs with a beautiful dark brown ground, and the octagonal ornament, the 'gul', displays small spikes).

The knotting is dense and very even on a foundation of wool; the pile is also wool.

62. Early Chinese Rug

A typical Chinese rug with a small selection of 'the hundred precious things' (see p. 38). The rug is woven with Senneh knots on a foundation of cotton, and has a woollen pile which is very deep and strong. The colour is blue and typical of many Chinese rugs. Note also the key pattern, and the broad, richly diapered main border.

63. Early Chinese Cock Rug

This rug is a charming example of a free pictorial design which would be most unusual in any oriental rug outside China. It is knotted with the Senneh knot on a foundation of cotton. The wollen pile is strong. The effect is brilliantly decorative; the design may be interpreted as two fancifully feathered cocks crowing at the red, rising sun.

64. Chinese Rug

Chinese rug-making is concentrated mainly in Peking, Shanghai, Tsingtao and Tientsin. This rug comes from one of the factory-like workshops of Tientsin. It is knotted with the Senneh knot on a strong foundation of cotton, and has a deep woollen pile. Chinese wool is very

Key and fret pattern borders

chine-spun in local factories. The rug is clipped in low relief.

Rugs of this type are made in various ground colours. Blue is the most common, but rose, yellow and beige are also used extensively. Often the design is constructed round a *shou*-like medallion (see p. 38) in the centre of the rug. The swastika pattern can be clearly distinguished in the border, which has been clipped to give an embossed effect. A number of standard qualities are made; they vary in price according to density and depth of pile. Modern Chinese rugs are remarkably cheap.

hard-wearing, and, therefore, particularly suitable for rugs. It is ma-

PRINCIPAL RUG-NAMES AND AREAS

Iranian Rugs

Northern Iran, also called Azerbaijan Group
Azerbaijan, Tabriz, Heriz, Goravan, Ardabil, Sarab, Mehriban, Bijar.

Western Iran, also called Kurdistan Group
Hamadan, Mosul, Lilihan, Maslaghan, Saveh, Feraghan, Saruck, Senneh, Seraband, Sultanabad, Mir, Luristan.

Southern Iran, also called Kirman Group
Kirman, Yezd, Raver, Abadeh, Bakhtiari, Qashgai, Shiraz, Afshar, Fars.

Eastern Iran, also called Khurasan Group
Khurasan, Meshed, Meshed Turkbaff.

Central Iran, also called Isfahan Group
Isfahan, Kashan, Joshaghan, Qum, Tehran, Nain.

The Turkoman Group

Bokhara (Yomud, Tekke, Salor), Arghan, Beshir, Panjde, Baluchi, Kachli, Samarkand.

Caucasian Rugs

North Caucasia
Daghestan, Derbend, Kuba, Soumak.
Trans-Caucasia
Kazak, Shirvan, Karabagh.

Turkish (Anatolian) Rugs

Western Turkey
Ghiordes, Bergama, Izmir (Smyrna), Kula, Melas, Oushak.
Central Turkey
Ladik, Konya, Mudjur.

Indian Rugs

West Pakistan
Karachi, Lahore.

Chinese Rugs

Peking, Tsingtao, Tientsin, Shanghai, Hongkong.

BIBLIOGRAPHY

Note: All the books mentioned below are in English, to help English and American readers, with one exception which contains a useful set of plates not found in any work in English.

W. von Bode and E. Kuhnel: *Near Eastern Carpets,* translated by Charles Grant Ellis, New York 1958.

Arthur Urbane Dilley: *Oriental Rugs and Carpets,* New York, new edition, 1959.

A. Cecil Edwards: *The Persian Carpet,* London 1953.

H. Haack: *Oriental Rugs an Illustrated Guide,* translated by G. and C. Wingfield Digby, London 1960.

Walter A. Hawley: *Oriental Rugs Antique and Modern,* New York, London and Toronto 1913.

Charles W. Jacobsen: *Oriental Rugs a Complete Guide,* Rutland, Vermont, and Tokyo 1962.

A. F. Kendrick and C. E. C. Tattersall: *Handwoven Carpets Oriental and European* (2 volumes), London 1922.

U. Schürmann: *Kaukasische Teppiche,* Braunschweig 1961.

A. B. Thacher: *Turkoman Rugs,* New York 1940 (Hajji Baba Club).

WHERE TO SEE ORIENTAL RUGS

There are important collections of antique oriental rugs in the Victoria and Albert Museum in London, The Metropolitan Museum of Art in New York, The Textile Museum and the Corcoran Gallery in Washington, The Los Angeles County Museum of Art and many other American collections. On the continent of Europe rugs may be seen especially in Vienna, *Österreichisches Museum für Angewandte Kunst,* Paris, *Musée des Arts Décoratifs,* Berlin, *Ehemals Staatlichen Museen,* Munich, *Bayerisches National Museum* and in collections of decorative arts in the museums of many other countries.

INDEX

INDEX OF NAMES

This index comprises all the *names* of oriental rugs found in the colour plates and the relevant descriptions. The *numbers* correspond to those of the colour plates and descriptions. Numbers in brackets indicate that the name is mentioned in the description only.

SUBJECT INDEX

This index consits of some *key-words,* with the number of the *page* on which the subject is mentioned. The names of oriental rugs occurring in the colour-plates and descriptions are included in the previous index of names.